Cuba, Adiós

Cuba, Adiós

A Young Man's Journey to Freedom

Lorenzo Pablo Martínez

Copyright © 2014 by Lorenzo Pablo Martínez

All rights reserved.

Names and identifying details of some people in this book have been changed to protect their privacy. Although all the stories are true, a few, those of a personal nature, were compressed or altered chronologically to help the flow of the narrative. Political events are presented accurately. The dialogue in the book is not meant to portray the exact words said by certain people. Rather, the author has tried to evoke the essence and meaning of what was said.

ASIN BOOL1MOL14

Jacket design by Ciro Flores

Printed in the United States of America

ISBN-13: 9781500952181

*To my parents because they had the vision
To Cris for lighting the way
To Thom for keeping me on the path*

Contents

Prelude   ix
First Movement
The Telegram   1
Chapter One   3
Chapter Two   12
Chapter Three   21
Chapter Four   29
Chapter Five   41
Chapter Six   50
Chapter Seven   66
Second Movement
Operación Pedro Pan: Becas
(Scholarships)   79
Chapter Eight   81
Chapter Nine   93
Chapter Ten   101
Chapter Eleven   110
Chapter Twelve   120
Chapter Thirteen   126
Chapter Fourteen   134
Chapter Fifteen   139
Chapter Sixteen   153
Chapter Seventeen   158
Chapter Eighteen   167

Third Movement
The Reunion   185
Chapter Nineteen   187
Chapter Twenty   197
Chapter Twenty-One   205
Chapter Twenty-Two   214
Chapter Twenty-Three   225
Chapter Twenty-Four   238
Coda   251
Operación Pedro Pan   262
Acknowledgement   267
About the Author   269

Prelude

"He was still too young to know that the heart's memory eliminates the bad and magnifies the good, and that thanks to this artifice we manage to endure the burden of the past."
—Gabriel García Márquez (*Love in the Time of Cholera*)

Trick the Moon

Walk, summer moon, walk.
Follow my steps. Stop and sigh.
Run when I say, Run!

As I played on *abuela's* long balcony, the evening wind slapped my face as if it were a disapproving parent. Chains around the base of two pots of pink geranium kept them secure to the balcony rail. The silvery glow bouncing off the building's facade made the shutters and door sparkle like brand new shoes. *Mamá, abuela,* and I had arrived earlier from Antilla via train; *el lechero* we called it, because it stopped everywhere like our milkman on his morning route. While *mamá* visited *la Doctora* next door I amused myself with a game of "Trick the Moon." The narrow street made the houses in front of *abuela's* balcony seem as if they were only inches away—I could almost touch them. I called it *abuela's* balcony, but it didn't belong to her. Not yet. It would be two more years before she would take over the place from her sister Concha.

The moon, sometimes skinny, sometimes full, sometimes near, sometimes far, showed a loyalty I expected from my playmates. Would it walk when I walked, stop when I stopped, run when I ran? Always! How did it know? "Is the moon God?" I asked. "Smart like your *abuela!*" she said with a wink.

I grew into a teenager, no longer interested in playing a "Trick-the-Moon" game. Instead, I would sit on a mahogany rocking chair with my elbows almost touching both sides of the balcony. I kept vigil over the two potted geranium plants that did not change over the years—same height, same fullness, same pink color—and shared with the moon secrets I couldn't tell anyone else. But, then, one day it all stopped. Moon, balcony, rocking chair, even the curious eyes from across-the street-neighbors, all stolen from me, like jewels embezzled by thieves at gun point.

It happened after my eighteenth birthday: the weapon a telegram. In their haste, the robbers shattered a snow globe that had housed my fantasy world; a world with the incandescent blue-green of Santiago's waters and cobblestone streets and buildings that dated back to a colonial past; a world that reflected the figure of Giselle whose ghost I believed lived in *Teatro Oriente* ever since I saw Alicia Alonso there in a spellbinding performance of the ballet; a world filled with the intensity of my piano lessons at the *Conservatorio Esteban Salas* and the reality of a music scholarship to Prague; a world that exposed times spent with Jorge Luis in a dark corner of *Parque Céspedes*, secretly wondering about the meaning of our friendship; a world that voiced the poetry of Martí and my own verses; a world that showed the figure of Fidel as leader of a revolution that supported my music; and most of all, a world that sparkled with the magic of the moon.

At the time, I did not know how much this telegram would turn my existence upside down, or that thousands of Cuban youngsters, my age and younger, had already received similar telegrams—the conveyors of exit permits that yanked us away from our families, our country, like weeds from a garden, and allowed us to enter the United States, unaccompanied. As overnight political orphans, we would face a future, vague and daunting—all in the name of freedom! That we would become part of history, a silent, unprecedented exodus of children to America, served as no consolation to us or the parents from whom we separated. Between the years 1960 and 1962, when many of these children should have been outside playing games with the moon or finding the magic inside their snow globes, more than 14,000 of them participated in a mass migration that became known as *Operación Pedro Pan*. Our mothers feared we would never return. Our fathers reassured us that we would—but to them *Peter Pan* was only a work of fiction. Each one of those children has a story. Here's mine.

First Movement
The Telegram

Chapter One

MEMORIES TEND to fade with the passage of time, but when an event affects a person's life in profound ways, it retains its vibrancy over the years. Although I admit to have examined documents related to my leaving Cuba (photographs, postcards, letters, newspaper articles) more times that I can possibly count, I don't need them as props to help me remember. All I have to do is close my eyes, and I'm there:

April 23, 1962
Our Pan American flight landed in Miami at 11:00 a.m., filled with the loud excitement of a future we had been promised but were unsure how to claim: scholarships, visas for our parents. The plane also carried a suitcase of secrets I had hoped would not make the trip. But there they were, ticking in my ear like a bomb ready to detonate.

While surrounding myself with a protective wall to keep my inner life hidden from Beni, my younger brother, we filled out forms that asked name, age, address in Cuba, and if anyone in our family had ever been a member of the Communist party. We filled out many of those; all asked the same things. Why so many? The answer spoke a language foreign to our ears. Every time we asked what was happening, we were told to wait.

Passengers whizzed through the immigration process and joined loved ones in a reunion of joy and tears; only Beni and I remained ensconced in the immigration waiting area. The two of us. Unaccompanied—no loved ones to welcome us with a hug or a kiss.

Fear robbed Beni's eyes of their honey-colored sparkle. "Do you know where we're going?" he asked, his voice quivering.

"A scholarship somewhere," I said, looking away to hide my own anxiety. I was just repeating what I'd heard in Cuba from *abuela, mamá* and *papá*. I was still unsure I believed it all.

"Like a boarding school?"

"Yes, like a boarding school."

"But where?"

My voice rose in pitch. "A boarding school!"

Responsibility had landed Beni on my shoulders; and his fourteen years felt like a Calvary already.

The immigration waiting area had a glass wall on one side, allowing people passing by to peek in. The lack of privacy felt as though I were undressing in front of an open window. Every wink, smile, or tear exposed itself without decorum. Because the chairs faced the glass, the only way to avoid the stare of that foreign world was standing and giving it our backs. Every time I rose, I did so as if exhausted by the experience. On the opposite side of the glass partition, in front of a concrete wall, a water cooler offered its reserves. Pasted above the cooler a poster of America's *Declaration of Independence* delivered words Beni tried to translate and memorize.

> *We hold these truths to be self-evident, that all men are created equal, that they are endowed by their Creator with*

certain unalienable Rights, that among these are Life, Liberty and the pursuit of Happiness.

To the right of the poster, a clock marked three in the afternoon. Four hours had passed since our arrival, and our stomachs growled as the seconds turned into minutes, the minutes into hours, and the hours piled on. We'd had nothing to eat since a pitiful breakfast that morning in Havana, and although we were here in pursuit of *life, liberty, and happiness*, it felt far from it.

We weren't allowed to leave the area, and even if we could, we had no money to buy anything. Our wealth consisted of three changes of clothes, two of them in our suitcases, and what we had on.

To pass the time and forget our hunger, I counted the blue plastic chairs and moved them in my head. Two over here, three over there, an asymmetrical design. Two facing two in courting fashion. I could see their elegant dance underscored by a Mozart minuet. Meanwhile Beni drained the water cooler as if he were a calf sucking milk from his mother.

During our wait, while Beni expressed his panic with unrelenting questions, I aired mine with a quiet that indicated a form of retreat, like a soldier defeated in battle. I had surrendered, despite my initial resistance to come to America, because of *papá's* anti-revolutionary activities. I feared for his life. Jorge Luís' indifference toward my leaving—in the past he had offered a *special friendship* I was often at a loss to describe—influenced my decision as well.

As I counted chairs, a woman dressed in a black skirt and white blouse approached me. The pink glow of her cheeks removed the whiteness of my despair. "Mr. O'Malley will see you shortly," she said in Spanish, her tone soft and reassuring. She spun around in a quiet rotation and with measured steps headed to and disappeared behind a green door.

As I watched the woman vanish, Beni, who had just come back from one of his trips to the water cooler said, "You must get me something to eat. If I drink any more water, I'm going to drown."

His words transported me back to a time when he almost drowned, a time I didn't know about secrets. Walking along the beach with me at her side, *mamá* was cradling Beni in her arms when she lost her footing, sending Beni, all of six months, flying into the water. I was short of three at the time. As in a scary fairy tale, the waves grew long, evil arms that refused to give him back for a long time. Everyone screamed, except me. "Let him go. We don't want him, anyway," I said.

Beni was an ugly blue when someone finally got him out. And, he was crying. Crying and spitting water all over.

Once we got him home, I remembered *mamá* singing a lullaby to him. I hated him then. Since she had sung the same lullaby to me before Beni was Beni, I thought it belonged to me and no one else.

As I glided over to Mr. O'Malley's office, I had a sense I might be the one slipping into deep, dark waters that would claim me forever. Who would sing me a lullaby? *"Duérmete mi niño, duérmete que yo...."*

A curtain of cigarette smoke propelled me backwards. I tried to enter a second time. "Here, here, take a seat," a smiling Mr. O'Malley said, pointing to the only available chair in the room. "Let's see what we can do for you." My eyes felt as if someone had thrown sand in them. I sneezed. Maybe I was allergic to the smoke, or the stench that betrayed an overflowing ashtray, or the smell of stale coffee coming from a mug on the desk. I wanted to open a window, but saw none. Mr. O'Malley, who seemed to enjoy touching his receding hairline as much as puffing on his cigarette, put his cigarette out. *Finally.*

"We need to fill out a few forms," Mr. O'Malley said.

Not again.

"It won't take long," he reassured me.

I would have preferred to turn my attention to a meal instead, although I would hardly admit this to Beni. On Mr. O'Malley's desk, a half-eaten apple looked appetizing, despite teeth marks and a certain discoloration from exposing its nakedness to the air for too long.

I worked on the forms.

"So, why are you here?" Mr. O'Malley asked.

What a stupid question! How would he react if I told him it was not Fidel I was running from?

"Not my idea," was all I could say.

"Our opportunity was Bay of Pigs," Mr. O'Malley said. "After that our chances were ruined. You wouldn't be here if we had gotten rid of Castro then."

I remembered *papá's* excitement when a group of around fourteen hundred Cuban exiles, trained in Guatemala with United States support, descended on our shores on April 17, the year before. *Papá* told everyone who'd listen that the brigade would receive aerial support from the Americans and that everyone throughout the island would revolt. In fact, *papá* created a mini revolt of his own in front of his business with signs that read, "Let's Welcome the U.S." He was fortunate to have escaped jail when the whole invasion failed. *Mamá* called it divine intervention, helped by prayers to her own *papá,* who seemed to come in handy at such moments.

Mr. O'Malley dialed a number. "No one answers." Pause. "Are you sure you don't have any relatives here to take you boys in?"

I opened my eyes wide. "We were promised a scholarship. Visas for our parents and sisters. We were—"

"You're jumping ahead. First we have to get you a place to stay. I don't know. Might have to separate you boys!"

What? My feet rattled the floor. My parents had instructed me to take care of Beni and now we were being threatened with separation? They had also promised their friends, the Guarches, would be at the airport to welcome us. But no one had shown up and we certainly could have used some help in dealing with this O'Malley guy.

Mr. O'Malley dialed a number again. Still no answer. He dialed a second time. "What's with this?" he said exasperated. "Nobody around? Has everyone gone to Cuba for another Bay of Pigs?"

His rant brought the attack back into focus. More than a thousand of the invaders found jail rather than the easy win they had expected, and less than forty-eight hours later Fidel addressed the nation declaring victory. The aftermath created tension in the island. Around two hundred thousand people were arrested, including members of the Catholic clergy. "Something went terribly wrong. Kennedy did not send the support he had promised," I remembered *papá* saying.

"Well, it's getting late. I don't think there's anything else I can do for you today." As he said this, Mr. O'Malley grabbed his name plate and put it in a drawer while he explained his shift was up. With arms above his head, he stretched his body in a big yawn, first to the left then the right. "Long day."

Long day? Sit on my chair, and you'll know how long long is. The thought of camping out at immigration played through my mind like an out-of-tune brass ensemble. Bay of Pigs had invaded me from head to toe, and I was on the losing side.

I got up so quickly I sent my chair flying to the floor, blocking the way out. The room went black, and then flashes of purple, blue, red, yellow blinded me. My body collapsed onto the floor.

Next thing I knew the doorknob turned several times and a woman's voice called from the other side.

"Charlie, Charlie, what's going on? Open up! Open up!" the voice said over repeated banging on the door.

"Look, maybe Jane can help you. I promised the honey to get home early. She's preparing a big feast. Our anniversary, you know."

"Charlie, what's going on? Open that door," the voice insisted.

"I'm being kept hostage by a zealous Cuban."

"I'm bringing security in and we're knocking down that door."

"You're not dead, are you?" Mr. O'Malley asked as he walked around my body, showing more concern for himself than for me.

"I'm fine. I'm fine," I said, slowly opening my eyes.

Getting up, I moved the chair out of the way, and the door opened. The same woman, who told me Mr. O'Malley would see me, came in. For the first time I noticed a string of pearls around her neck that reminded me of *abuela's*.

"You must have fainted," she said, the ocean of her eyes looking straight at me.

"Juana, I told him there was nothing I could do for him today."

"How old?" she asked.

"Seventeen," Mr. O'Malley said.

"Eighteen," I corrected him.

"Did you call Matecumbe?" she asked.

"No answer. He comes with a younger brother. Fourteen. Don't think we can keep them together. Matecumbe, I'm sure, won't take both…and none of the other camps will either."

I didn't know what all this Matecumbe business meant and I was unaware that its mere mention exposed me for the first time to a program Beni and I would end up participating in: *Operación Pedro Pan*.

Out of a skirt pocket, Jane produced a handkerchief. "Here, dampen this with cold water," she ordered O'Malley.

"I guess they were not expecting anyone today," he said. He took a few steps out the door, then poked his head back in.

"Wasn't that area filled with coral reefs? How could we overthrow him?" I guessed he was not finished with Bay of Pigs.

"Make it cold!" Jane said forcefully. Mr. O'Malley hurried out. I couldn't understand his fascination with Bay of Pigs. I was here to discuss my future, not what had gone wrong with that infamous attack.

With Jane's help, I sat on the chair, rearranging the weight of my body. I noticed her figure outlined soft curves, the type Latin women are proud to show off. Her name was Juana, known here by the American name of Jane.

"Don't worry, we'll get you out of here. Something to eat too. You must be hungry."

I didn't answer.

My thoughts fluttered like butterflies, going from flower to flower to feed on their nectar. So swift was their flight, though, that I could barely grab the wing of one memory before another appeared. Then a clear picture. A telephone number dormant in my pants pocket. Why had I forgotten?

So used was I to keeping secrets that this one had become just one more. I would grab that butterfly. That butterfly would fly us out of a hell that only days before I didn't expect to find myself in.

Chapter Two

WHEN BENI and I arrived in Miami, I was unaware the daily influx of Cubans fleeing Castro's regime was already turning the city into another Ellis Island. How had we ended up as another statistic, two young Cubans seeking political asylum, when my parents' relationship with Fidel had started as an idyllic love story?

The *courtship* began when Fidel, his brother Raúl, and a group of around one hundred and twenty men attacked the Moncada Barracks in Santiago on July 26, 1953, at the closing of the city's yearly carnival—the date gave name to Fidel's revolution: *Movimiento 26 de Julio*. The timing was auspicious. While the city focused on the festivities—*comparsas* (groups of dancers and musicians) performed choreographed steps, mostly to a conga beat, and beer flowed freely through the crowds like river down a mountain—Fidel prepared a *comparsa* of his own. As lead choreographer, he instructed his revolutionaries to infiltrate the compound, seal it, take over the post's radio station and broadcast an appeal urging others to join his dance—*the insurrection*. His plan failed, and although most of Fidel's rebels were killed, if not in action, under torture, the ideals behind the bold attack galvanized the country into underground resistance and eventually open action against the existing regime. Fidel, Raúl and a handful of others escaped, but were later captured and tried. At the trial, in which he represented himself, Fidel showed his gift for oratory in a four-hour discourse that justified his actions and ended with the line *History Will Absolve Me*. When in admiration *papá* quoted from the speech, the words had no resonance. I was nine years old at the time.

For the attack on the Moncada, Fidel and others in his group received terms of up to fifteen years. Two years after the assault, however, then President Fulgencio Batista, thinking that Fidel was no longer a threat, released him from jail. Fidel left for Mexico, but later with a group of eighty-two supporters that included his brother Raúl and Ché Guevara, he returned to Cuba on the *Granma* yacht.

The journey was perilous. The boat could comfortably accomodate 12 passengers, and because of the overload, the large group was also carrying food, fuel for a week and weapons, the vessel began to leak; at one point it looked like it might sink. The fact that the engines were in total disrepair and needed constant attention added to the group's travails. Food had to be rationed and many of the passengers became sick during the rough 1,200 mile voyage—there was little room for anyone to rest. Miraculously, the group reached shore, but there, they suffered serious losses at the hands of Batista's army. Only about a dozen of Fidel's revolutionaries at last reached the Sierra Maestra Mountains, from which, with a meager supply of weapons and little food, they waged a relentless, and, ultimately, victorious war against Batista.

Although most people associate the revolution with men, Fidel, Raúl, Ché, Camilo Cienfuegos, many women joined Fidel's forces in the mountains and fought alongside their male counterparts. Among them were Celia Sánchez, who allegedly was Fidel's mistress, and Vilma Espín, who met Raúl in Mexico before the Granma expedition and eventually became his wife.

While Fidel was in the mountains, my parents offered support, sheltering rebels in our home and helping to acquire and transport arms to the revolutionaries—dressed in a nun's habit, *mamá* was able to get past Batista's men posted at various points. During this time, conversations at our house were held *sotto voce*—the muted sounds presented an anomaly, since most Cubans are known for speaking in two settings: loud and louder.

Among the youth joining Fidel in the Sierra Maestra was my seventeen-year-old cousin, Adolfito, *mamá's* sister's son, who, after the revolution's victory, was rewarded with an important post in Fidel's government. That he remained loyal to the revolution much after our family had turned against it created a schism, *mamá* the most affected by it. After all, she had raised him as her own son after my aunt divorced. "Fidel has poisoned your mind," she'd tell him.

The long *engagement* culminated in a *wedding announcement*, when Batista fled the country on New Year's Eve, 1958, and next day Fidel declared himself leader of the new Cuba. The mood in the island was celebratory; music played everywhere; impromptu dancing broke out on street corners; Cubans, dressed in red and black, the colors of Fidel's revolutionary flag, cheered *el barbudo* (the bearded one) with boisterous toasts of beer and rum.

The groom was ready to marry, and as he rode the streets from Oriente to Havana, throngs of people greeted the *matrimonial car*, pouring out of windows, balconies and rooftops, chanting, "*Fidel, Fidel, Fidel*" in tones that verged on the religious. But then, many at the time believed this was no simple *groom* but the *Messiah*, sent to deliver the island from the evils of Batista's dictatorship: corruption that had plagued the highest levels of government. "We'll finally have a democracy in Cuba," I remembered *papá* saying. Soon, he'd take back those words.

The ink on the marriage certificate was barely dry when signs the union was doomed emerged. The elections Fidel promised were never held, and death by firing squad (*el paredón*) became commonplace. At first these executions were intended for members of the previous regime. Before long, anyone who criticized the new government, including some who had helped Fidel gain power, risked jail or the firing squad; rumors about Fidel being a Communist, which he denied at first, added to the mistrust.

For parents, an all-out panic alarm went off when Fidel closed every school in the country, public and private, to start a comprehensive educational reform; sent close to 1,000 students to Russia; turned a few military posts into schools that many believed were indoctrination centers; and started an "illiteracy eradication" campaign that sent thousands of people into the countryside to teach *campesinos* (peasants) how to read—many were young girls, who *unchaperoned* came back pregnant. Then there was *patria potestad,* a rumor about the government's intention to remove children from their homes to be educated in the revolution's mores. A copy of a document outlining such plan ended up in *mamá's* hands.

"They want to take over the education of our children, brainwash them," *mamá* would say through trembling lips, her eyes, at those times, open but not seeing, her hands, one on top of the other, pushing down on her chest as if to prevent it from exploding. The revolution she had loved and supported had become her nemesis; *papá* shared her feelings.

For me, the closing of schools meant something different. As a child I studied piano in Antilla and later went to

Santiago for lessons with *tía* Chuchi (an accomplished pianist) and occasionally Raúl (a friend of *tía's* who had gained national recognition as a performer and teacher). After the revolution's triumph, when the *conservatorio* opened and Raúl was hired to teach the advanced piano students, I didn't hesitate to move to Santiago to study with him.

I didn't see myself as a flag-waving *Fidelista*, except perhaps on the day of the revolution's victory when the country's enthusiasm washed over me and I joined the cheers of those who welcomed the new regime. With schools closed, I had the type of world I had always envisioned: lessons at the *conservatorio*, attending concerts, meeting exciting artists. A perfect life.

At this time, I met Jorge Luís, who worked for *la Casa de Cultura*, an organization created by Fidel to oversee all cultural activities in Santiago. Our friendship, which had started as a comfortable interaction with someone who admired my playing, grew into feelings on my part of trust and platonic intimacy that were as exciting as they were confusing.

Jorge Luís often joined me when, with a group from the *conservatorio*, I performed in government-sponsored recitals in nearby towns. He also introduced me to celebrated artists, such as classical pianists Ivette Hernández and Zenaida Manfugás; singer Pedrito Rico, nicknamed the "Angel of Spain"; performance artist Luís Carbonell, and celebrated star of film and television, Libertad Lamarque. By far, the most exciting performer he introduced me to was internationally renowned ballerina Alicia Alonso. As a wide-eyed sixteen-year-old who had never seen in person a full-length ballet or any length ballet for that matter, my meeting Alonso would become a transformative experience that resonates to this day.

It was 1960, two years before I left for Miami. As I stood in the lobby of the *conservatorio*, I was overcome by the image in front of me.

The hair, black and pulled back into a small bun, shimmered. The red lips widened into a smile. The patrician nose pointed up and led the way. Alicia Alonso had just made an entrance at the *conservatorio*. Behind her walked husband Fernando—they were still married at the time—and Jorge Luís, representing *Casa de Cultura*.

The Alonsos had brought their ballet company to Santiago for a week of performances and wanted *dos muchachos* to appear in the "mad scene" of *Giselle*. The relatively new group could not afford to waste its limited number of male dancers on non-dancing roles.

Dancing with Alicia? The ballerina who had spent several seasons with the Ballet Russes de Monte Carlo dancing with Igor Youskevitch? Jorge Luís nodded.

"I don't…don't dan-ce!" I stuttered.

"I don't expect you to do a *grand jeté*," she said.

"A what?"

"Push off the floor with one leg, jump in the air, high, high, high, and land on the other leg." Although she demonstrated with barely a hint of the movement, she looked like a bird taking flight. "Just walk. Walk like a dancer." Then, she walked, toes pointed, as if she were stepping on a bed of clouds.

Although Cuban-born, Alicia had initially come to the public's attention in the United States, first on the chorus line of a Broadway musical and later as one of the stars of Lucia Chase's Ballet Theatre. She had gained critical notice and fan adulation for her precise technique and the dramatic flair she brought to her roles. While keeping an active performing schedule, Alicia had maintained a ballet company in Cuba, the *Alicia Alonso Ballet Company*, which she visited regularly and kept afloat with her own financial resources and the help of wealthy friends. Batista, aware of her opposition to his regime, offered little support.

On a trip to Havana, *tía* Chuchi had seen Alicia perform. "She's ethereal. As Giselle, she doesn't dance as much as she floats."

I had read that *Giselle* and *Swan Lake* were two ballets Alicia had performed in the Soviet Union, the first Western ballerina to have the honor. When Fidel came to power, he asked her to start her own school and, unlike Batista, offered annual financial support. It was this group, named the *Ballet Nacional de Cuba*, the Alonsos had brought to Santiago.

As I participated in rehearsals, I learned what few outside of Alicia's inner circle knew—Alicia the ballerina was almost blind. After three operations, two of them unsuccessful, and a third after which she had to stay in bed motionless for a year, she had only partial sight in one eye and no periphery vision.

Alicia herself coached me. With my arm around her waist, and butterflies that threatened a stampede in my stomach, we walked around the stage to Adolphe Adam's lilting *Giselle* score. "No, no, too hard," she said without as much as a glance in my direction. "Pointed toes, and softer, softer. Better. Better!"

Once satisfied, she went on with the rest of the rehearsal. Instead of dancing she mimed her steps while talking. "*Pirouette, pirouette,* turn, turn, *glissade, glissade, glissade,* glide, glide, glide, *grand jeté, grand jeté,* then, lift...lift...lift...no, no!"

Music stopped. Dancers froze. All stared at her.

"You have to be over there. Exactly three feet from me," she admonished her partner. Once in a while, she screamed,

"Those lights. Those lights have to be brighter. Brighter. You want me to fall into the pit?"

"I'm taking care of it, Alicia." Her husband reassured her.

Seated next to me while we watched rehearsals, a member of her company whispered, "Her partner must be exactly where she needs him…footlights? They have to be strong so she knows if she's too close to the pit."

Then came performance time.

During the mad scene, her abandon into the psychosis of her character had genius written all over: she twirled, jumped, danced on point, achieving such height on her *grands jetés*, she looked as if wires suspended her. When she exited into the wings, someone was there to catch her and place her exactly where she had to appear next. Once back on stage, she was Alicia, the great ballerina. She needed no support. Dancing lived inside her and what she saw inside she shared with the world.

At the end of each ballet, Alicia's bows turned into choreographed performances. She took flowers from a fan; held them to her bosom; curtsied deeply to the audience; looked up toward the balcony, and then straight ahead, an arm extended to recognize her dancing partner. From her bouquet, she offered him a rose, which she kissed first. After many more curtseys, to her partner, then the audience, she exited to the wings.

The public adored her, clapping non-stop. And Alicia never tired of re-emerging to acknowledge the applause.

After the performance, at a banquet in her honor, I didn't want to let go of the magic of Alicia, so I went up to her. I tapped her gently on the shoulder. Would she recognize me? She turned toward me. Her red lips moved. "My lovely dancing partner!" she said. Then, from a bouquet she had placed on the table in front of her, she took a red rose, kissed it, and handed it to me. To Jorge Luís she gave an autographed photo of herself as *Giselle,* a picture he hung in his office.

By then her revolutionary fervor and artistic brilliance had gained her iconic status in Fidel's Cuba. To all, she was beauty; she was dance; she was Alicia. To me she was my dancing partner!

Years later at a performance in New York City of *A Chorus Line,* a musical based on a group of dancers auditioning for a show, I heard one of the characters sing how, as a little girl, ballet had helped her cope with a difficult home life. My eyes filled with tears. I recalled Alicia. Like the song, the world she had exposed me to, thanks to Jorge Luís, was magical and "beautiful." This was the world I had refused to leave, a world I couldn't convince my parents I belonged to.

Chapter Three

MY PARENTS' discontent with the revolution had turned into an all-out effort to leave the country; some of their plans were at best mad, like the scheme to have me escape via the Guantánamo base. I was to stand in a pre-determined corner of Santiago, where I would wait for a *connection* to drive me to a spot that separated the American army base from the Cuban side, allegedly a remote section of the fence unguarded by Cuban armed forces. Once inside, I would ask for asylum for the rest of the family.

When the brain behind the scheme met death, taking a group to that same *unpatrolled* area a week before my scheduled date, the plot failed; we learned of the man's unfortunate fate in the paper. Although marred in blood, the disaster didn't stop my parents from investigating other ways to leave the country, particularly getting *me* out. They insisted that if I stayed, because of my sympathy for the regimen, I would end up marching in the military, or possibly getting killed at the hands of a revolution that would turn unforgiving if it learned of my parents' subversive activities. Getting visas to leave legally for the United States was difficult after the United States broke diplomatic relations with Cuba in 1961, and the American Embassy in Havana closed its doors. Many had seen their opportunities to leave the island shattered, but even after the Guantánamo plans failed, my parents continued on their quest. "Children are leaving, anyway," *mamá* pleaded with Sister Margarita, a friend of hers, certain that through the Church she would get American visas for her children. "Just no one talks about it...No one will tell you...Such a secret. How do they do it? You must tell me, you must tell me. Please help us. Help us!" Those words, which *mamá* repeated when she spoke of her visit to her friend, pounded on my brain like a boxer's fists. The second time *mamá* visited Sister Margarita, I insisted on accompanying her.

"I just want to be there to hear what you talk about... how you plan my life without my consent."

"You have to stay quiet," *mamá* insisted.

"Of course," I said without any intention of keeping my promise.

As we entered the front gate of *La Colonia Española*, we met three nuns whose faces looked familiar but whose names I didn't know. We walked up the hill, past the palms and the jasmines, and made a left toward the children's pavilion, the first building in the clinic's vast complex, a health facility run by the Sisters of Charity.

We entered the children's wing and walked up the narrow, circular stair to the second floor, where *mamá* asked for Sister. A young nun, barely in her twenties, with small, gold-rimmed glasses asked us to wait in the Sister's office. The mellifluous chanting of the rosary coming from the chapel down the hall reached our ears.

Sister Margarita's office displayed a desk next to a large window and a couple of chairs. On the desk rested a gold crucifix and prayer book. Through the window, the sun sneaked in as though it were a house burglar trying to avoid detection. *Mamá* walked over to the window and looked out at the familiar buildings that converged around a central plaza. I joined her there, my gaze pausing at a wall of purple and red bougainvillea that served as backdrop for a statue of the *Virgen de Guadalupe*. In front of the statue, patients and families sat on stone benches. I remember sitting there myself during a stay at *la Colonia* to have my appendix removed when I was ten years old. As the scene re-arranged itself, with people walking away and some claiming a bench, I thought of what we had already encountered on our way here.

Minutes after leaving *abuela's* apartment, *mamá* and I stood on the corner of Hartman and Heredia, waiting for the light to change, when we heard, "Tica, where are you going, so pretty?"
We recognized the voice, a husky sound belonging to Josefa, *abuela's* across-the street-neighbor, and once one of *mamá's* closest friends. The words sounded sarcastic rather than inquisitive. At once, *mamá* hunched her shoulders, the way a knee responds when its reflexes are tested. I could tell she wanted to erase her poise from her physical self, to erase herself, ourselves, from this corner, where Josefa, a half-smoked cigar dangling from her lips, greeted us.
Mamá bypassed a hello kiss and simply acknowledged her friend with a half-smile. Josefa sported a wrinkled, green militia uniform, a look she accented with heavy, military boots and hair tied back into a sloppy pony tail. *Mamá* later said she hardly recognized in that revolutionary persona the beauty queen who used to spend innumerable hours pampering herself with mud baths or designing and making her own clothes to keep in step with the latest fashion.

"Look at you, as beautiful as ever," Josefa said, looking at *mamá* as if inspecting a rare piece of art. Then, pointing at *mamá*'s handbag, she added, "Anything subversive there?"

Mamá's body stiffened. "Compact and lipstick. What can be more subversive than that?"

"Oh, Tica, your humor always saves you."

A chuckle made its way from *mamá's* lips, disappearing almost as soon as it announced itself to the world.

I didn't know then the content of *mamá's* handbag, but I knew the story of *mamá's* friendship with Josefa well. Starting in boarding school, it had continued until recently when their opposing political views erected a tall fence between the two that neither seemed able to trespass. Stubborn Josefa. Or, was it *mamá* the one who remained unyielding?

They were thirteen years old when they first met. Ileana, who would later become Sister Margarita, was also part of the devilish triad the girls immediately formed, raising hell everywhere they went, serving tea laced with vinegar to an unsuspecting girl, helping someone with the homework, and while one of them (usually Ileana) would expound on Einstein's theory of relativity, the others would spill Coca-Cola on the girl's bed.

"Tica, you don't call me Pepa, any more." Hurt colored her words.

She was right. The nickname, Pepa, hardly came out of *mamá's* mouth any more. She had discarded it from her vocabulary for fear it would take the two friends to an unwelcome place, a place that would be different, dangerous, according to *mamá*. While *mamá* returned to Antilla after boarding school, Josefa, remained in Santiago with her family, and the two remained in touch over the years. Lately, however, their interaction had been sporadic.

As we stood facing Josefa, the sound of an approaching parade reached us. A group of boys, dressed in olive green uniforms with red bandanas around their necks, had turned the corner and was heading in our direction. I figured the youngest to be around eight, the oldest no more than twelve or thirteen. Traffic stopped to let the boys pass. As they marched, three deep, the boys chanted, "*Patria o Muerte, venceremos. Patria o Muerte, venceremos.*" (Give us liberty or give us death.)

A wall of curious spectators formed around us, pinning us to our spots. While the onlookers applauded in support of the marchers and chanted along (Josefa perhaps the most enthusiastic), *mamá* stayed silent, clutching her purse in a tight hold; I knew she didn't want her children to participate in anything like this. "Politics is not for the young," she had said many times.

Once the marchers disappeared and their revolutionary chant faded, pedestrians resumed their intentions, walking away from us. Without uttering a word, we crossed the street. *Mamá's* eyes looked teary, probably because she knew the distance we were gaining over Josefa was one they would never bridge again.

When the clicking of heels against the austere marble floor announced Sister Margarita's arrival, *mamá* and I turned around.

Sister stopped short of the room, a dramatic entrance if I'd ever seen one. Only her black shoes and bottom of her long white habit came into view. She used the doorframe as a prop, the way a performer uses a stage curtain to flirt with the audience; then she entered, full face, with the intensity of a flamenco dancer. When she was a young girl, Sister Margarita, Ileana as she was then, wanted to be a flamenco dancer along the lines of Carmen Amaya. According to *mamá*, her skills with the castanets were unsurpassed. A brush of the hand now, a movement that seemed perfectly choreographed and rehearsed, sent Sister's white habit billowing behind. *Indeed, she could have been another Amaya.*

"Tica, my precious flower," Sister said. Then she acknowledged me. "And my dear Loren."

"Much wilted today," *mamá* said.

"Nonsense, you're radiant. Always. Even in my old dull habits. How you fooled those Batista's men!"

As she kissed *mamá*, Sister was careful to keep her starched headdress out of the way. "Loren, how's that piano?" I offered a hint of a smile.

"Sister, I want to show you." *Mamá* pulled out a piece of paper from her purse and handed it over. Sister Margarita put her eyeglasses on, sat at the desk, and read aloud. "Children will remain with their parents until they are three years old…then they'd be the charge of the state…Hmm… *patria potestad*. I hope no one knew you were carrying this."

My heart thumped so loud, they must have heard it. No wonder *mamá* seemed nervous when Josefa asked about the handbag.

Allegedly signed by Fidel, the document outlined his intentions to have all children live in government housing so they could be educated in the revolution's ideals without parental interference.

"Ran into Pepa, Josefa," *mamá* corrected herself.

"Don't hear from her these days."

"Imagine. Living in government housing," *mamá* said, her body trembling. "Sure, they'd be allowed to visit their families two days a month."

"Great concession!" Sister Margarita said and continued to read, now silently.

"Where did you get that? It's gossip. You know it's not true." My words thundered.

"Loren, you promised."

Slowly, Sister Margarita folded the document and gave it back to *mamá*. "You have reasons to be concerned. I'm not sure you should be walking around with this, though."

"Sister, you should have seen what we just saw. '*Patria o Muerte, venceremos.*' Children chanting. Young boys willing to die for the revolution. You've got to help us. You've got to help us. We need to get the boys out before they are recruited—"

"But, I'm not marching anywhere. I'm with the *conservatorio*."

"As you know there is no way to get a visa, a regular visa," Sister said, playing with the crucifix as if it were a tile in a domino game.

"You had mentioned you'd look into..." *Mamá's* words trailed off.

"There is hope. The U.S. is letting children in. A special permit. Something called Visa Waiver."

"How do we get it?" *mamá* asked.

"Granted to children between the ages of three and sixteen. Loren is over the age limit," Sister said, picking up the crucifix once again. She got up, walked over to the window, and then turned to face us. By then, tears had flooded *mamá's* face.

"Clementina tells me I'll be destroying the family," *mamá* said.

"Let your sister listen to her own heart."

I gave a sigh of relief. I was too old for a children's visa. I was unaware then of the secretive efforts, growing by the day, to airlift children out of Cuba, and the fact that exemptions could be made for those over the age of sixteen wishing to leave. That's why, a year later when a government telegram arrived announcing my departure, I was as stunned as if I had been told I was adopted. The world as I knew it had collapsed.

Chapter Four

April 20, 1962

THE SUN slipped through the glass window of the practice room like an uninvited listener. Raúl and I had just finished working on Mozart's C Major Piano concerto, a piece I'd already played in public with Raúl on the second piano and that I would perform again in three weeks—this time with a small chamber orchestra.

Raúl closed the music. "You're well prepared," he said.

"Yes?" I asked, my tone begging for reassurance. I dropped my gaze to the shadows created on the floor by the intrusive sun. Something about their dance made me uneasy.

"You can't let doubts consume you," Raúl said. "It's Mozart, Mozart, Mozart, until then."

My anxiety reflected the significance of the concert, billed as a strategic step toward a piano scholarship to Prague. A concert to loud applause and congratulatory flowers would secure the scholarship: a year or two of studies in Czechoslovakia, after which I'd return to Santiago to continue coaching with Raúl. A less than triumphant performance, on the other hand, would mean…well, I wasn't sure what it would mean. Certainly, it would brand me as a failure, and the revolution didn't like losers.

But Raúl said I was well prepared and I trusted him. My admiration for him as a mentor and my respect for his artistry had not wavered since the first time I met him. I was seven years old then.

"*¿Está muy lejos?*" I asked *tía* Chuchi as we walked through narrow streets over tracks meant for street cars.

"*¡Qué va!* We're almost there. Don't be scared."

"I'm not."

"It's just a visit. *Una visita.* He'll talk. He loves to talk… you'll play a little…maybe he'll play."

Tía Chuchi had known Raúl since childhood, and she wanted to show me off to her friend. They had met when they were both students of Cervera's, a respected pianist and composer, originally from Barcelona, who had opened a music school in Santiago. Later, Raúl went to New York to continue his studies, eventually studying with the renowned Chilean pianist, Claudio Arrau.

Raúl kept all the windows in his living room closed to prevent the outside world from interfering with his music making. The resulting darkness, compounded by an unapologetic layer of dust covering most of the furniture, gave the room an eerie feeling. The one shiny piece of furniture was an upright Steinway piano, although the top was partially covered by a hand-embroidered Spanish shawl he had acquired during a trip to Spain. I found out Raúl employed a cleaning lady, when she appeared at some point during our visit with a plate of cookies and glasses of fresh lemonade.

Raúl shared with us his scrapbook of press clippings, reading a few lines from some: "His effortless virtuosity and interpretative skills were tested to great success with his reading of the B-flat minor…" Despite his ardent protestations, and my few years, I realized Raúl quite enjoyed the praise.

I asked him why he lived in Santiago. After brushing back hair from his forehead he responded, "Santiago is the perfect place for me. Not big, not small. I play here. I teach. A little travel here and there. And I'm never away from family for long." Family included an elderly mother and a sister, both of whom lived with him in a part of the house I never saw. "One day, Santiago will be the place for you," he told me.

At *tía's* request, Raúl agreed to play. He walked over to the piano, sat down, and suddenly Chopin's Sonata in B-flat minor, the subject of one of his reviews, came to life. His elegant posture and exciting technique mesmerized me. I had never heard anything like it in person. The room vibrated with the melodies of Chopin and I wanted to open the windows to let the world in on the magic of his playing. I knew the galloping sounds of the opening well and could hum the entire first movement, after having listened to a Rubinstein recording over and over in my room until *mamá* forbade me to play it again. As Raúl continued, I imagined Chopin playing for friends, his fingers dashing through the same masterpiece; I wondered if dust would have covered the furniture, as well. After the first movement, Raúl turned to *tía*, who was clapping enthusiastically, and then to me. I was in such awe, I made no sound.

"Well, your turn," he said to me. "What do you want to play?"

"That," I said without hesitation.

"Of course, my little Chopin. Someday, someday."

At the time, I lived with my parents in Antilla, so studying with this giant of the piano was out of the question. As a teenager, however, I traveled to Santiago, a city that exposed me to a cultural life I'd not experienced before; and after the revolution's triumph, I moved there to enter the conservatorio where Raúl had been put in charge of teaching the advanced students.

Leaving my hometown of Antilla had produced no tears. Situated on the northeastern side of the island, Antilla was built like a balcony over one of the biggest bays in the world. Despite enjoying a spectacular view, the city was Santiago's poor cousin with none of Santiago's vibrancy. Antilla had three major streets and no cultural life to speak of. It thrived on gossip. Who was sleeping with whom? Who got pregnant out of wedlock? Who had a deviant sexual orientation? Who supported the revolution? Who had betrayed it?

Santiagueros, on the other hand, cared about the latest concert, art exhibition, visiting artists, exciting authors, a perfect place to get lost in and offer one's secrets to the moon.

My weekly sessions with Raúl in a colonial building that was the birthplace of Cuban poet José María Heredia felt like regular visits to a museum. Every room in Heredia's house, now the *conservatorio,* resonated with his writings. I could almost hear his voice reciting his own poetry, and his footsteps tapping behind Czerny exercises and Chopin Etudes that echoed through the rooms.

In that setting my piano lessons were as inspiring as they were comfortable, and the possibility they might end, if I received the scholarship, made me anxious. But Raúl encouraged me. He had studied abroad and thought a similar experience would benefit me. Despite my apprehension—I had never been to a foreign country away from family—the prospects of Prague appealed to this eighteen-year-old. Jorge Luís too encouraged the idea.

After Raúl said, "It's Mozart, Mozart, Mozart until then," I left the *conservatorio,* with music vibrating through every molecule of my body. It was the music of a concerto with an expansive first movement; an andante of inspiring beauty; and a lighthearted final movement reminiscent of the *opera buffa* Mozart was fond of using in his finales.

I reached Enramada, the most commercial street in Santiago. People buzzed about like bees, crisscrossing the street from one side to the other, carrying big and small packages. I clutched only Mozart's melodies.

Fa, la, do, la si, fa, mi, mi re.

When I arrived at Hartmann 507, I took the marble steps, two by two, to the second floor apartment where *abuela* lived. "Mozart, Mozart, Mozart." Raúl's words still echoed in my head.

Mi, re, re, mi, re, re, mi re, re, si.

When I entered, I found an almost limp body rocking away its life in a quiet, semi-dark corner of the living room; all shutters were closed. *Abuela* looked ashen-faced, as if she had just seen the ghost of *abuelo*, who had been dead since I was five.

"*Si Ernesto estuviera vivo, ¿qué diría? ¿qué diría?*"

"*Abuela*, he's dead. What are you talking about? What have you seen?"

"*Ay, Loren, mi vida, te vas.* You and Beni."

Mi, fa, la, fa, re, do, si, do.

"Where, where are we going?"

La, sol, la, do, la, sol.

"*Tu papi y tu mami ya lo saben.*"

"What are you talking about, what do *mami* and *papi* know? Tell me, what is it?"

At that moment *abuela* produced from one of her pockets the infamous telegram, and while I stared at the unlit brass and porcelain chandelier that hung from the center of the room, she gunned me down with instructions, delivered almost in one breath. I was to take the last train of the day to Antilla. From there *mamá, papá,* my brother, Beni, and I would go to Havana; and from Havana, Beni and I would fly to Miami. My sisters Betty and Tere, lacking their own American visas, would stay in Antilla, so as not to raise suspicion from nosy neighbors.

By then, the music that had followed me to *abuela's* apartment had been replaced by fear, the kind children have for monsters lurking under their beds. The monster showed its full face in *abuela's* hands. Although small, and yellow, its threat loomed as large as the giant lizard that had tormented many of my childhood dreams.

Abuela folded the telegram and placed it in her pocket carefully, as if she were putting an expensive piece of jewelry back into its padded box. Even tucked away, it still confirmed Beni's and my departure. Stop. He and I the only ones leaving. Stop. Unaccompanied. Stop. No other family member. Stop. Just the two of us. Exile in America. Such a blessing! Stop, stop, stop!

I emphasized what *abuela* already knew: the concert around the corner, ready to show its bright face, and the music scholarship to Prague that depended on that performance. I could not believe Fidel's government would send a telegram granting me permission to leave the country when it knew of my concert and future scholarship to Prague.

Abuela mentioned the fun we would have in America, the cities we would visit, the scholarships waiting for us. When I questioned her about the scholarships ("Where, for how long, what kind?"), her response was silence.

After a few seconds, words came to her. "God will help you." But I didn't want God to help me. I wanted to know the what, when, and where of all this nonsense.

I wondered what my options were. How could I go against what I'd just heard, against *abuela*?

Abuela was almost a figure of fiction, running her house as if she were ruling over a sugar plantation, the *dueña* dispatching orders to employees, relatives, even friends with stubborn determination. No one contradicted her—ever.

Abuela was old before she was old; ever since I remembered, her hair was white gathered at the nape of her neck, her dress black, her wire-rimmed glasses, small and round. Something about her never got old: her posture. It seemed to get more erect as the years went by, giving her an intimidating air some found arrogant.

At three in the afternoon, without fail, she would dress up, pearls and all, and be ready to receive. In Santiago, in all of Cuba, friends showed up without announcing their visit beforehand. *Abuela* was always ready! When a visitor arrived, the interaction would go something like this:

"*Don Francisco, ¿un pedacito de cake?*"

"*No, Lucila, imposible.*" I could not have a piece of cake.

"*Pero no me puede hacer ese desprecio.*" You can't turn me down like that.

"*Ay, por favor, Doña, no, no puedo.*" I can't, really!

"*Sí, como no…con un cafecito.*" With a little coffee, you'll see.

"*Bueno, bueno, si usted insiste. Pero una cosita de nada.*" If you insist, but a small piece.

"*Por supuesto.*" Of course.

For Don Francisco, or anyone else, to accept food without a bit of resistance would have been considered vulgar. I loved listening to *abuela's* back and forth with her visitors as they negotiated her offer of something to eat and drink.

Now, I had to negotiate something other than a piece of cake: my future. But, how? I could go back to the *conservatorio* and see Raúl. Or call Jorge Luís. But the only phone in the house sat on a wood credenza in the dining room, an area connected to the living room by a small hallway. Although *abuela* obscured my view somewhat, I could see the table already set for lunch: china, crystal, freshly-starched napkins, and the silver bell *abuela* always rang to call everyone to the table. Francisca was placing platters on the table. Although she had seen me, she avoided my gaze. A Haitian woman of undetermined age, Francisca sported a nose that spanned two continents and a smile that hinted at secrets never revealed. I wondered if she already knew the secret of the telegram. Francisca had worked for *abuela* since before I was born. I didn't want Francisca, or *abuela* for that matter, to hear my conversation with Jorge Luís. As an employee of *La Casa de Cultura*, he knew about the scholarship to Prague (in fact he had been working behind the scenes to make it happen). Was he aware of the telegram as well? It had come from the government, and he worked for... No, no, not possible. He couldn't have known. He would have contacted me, warned me about it.

"Francisca has made a wonderful *arroz con pollo*," *abuela* said, her tone flat. "How she managed to get a chicken, I don't know."

"I'm not hungry," I said, still frozen in place. I searched *abuela's* face, hoping to find understanding behind one of her wrinkles. "You want me to give up Prague. Everything neat, taken care of, trip, lessons, all in exchange for Miami, a strange, hazy, uncertain future?" I asked, as tears I had stifled before flooded my face. "Besides," I added, "this revolution is here to stay...and I like it!"

"How can you say that? Fidel has let us all down. Can't you see? He's not the saint you think he is. He's a Fascist...a..."

Hijo de puta? I knew what she wanted to say was "son-of-a-bitch." But such expression would never touch *abuela's* lips.

Instead, after a long pause, she said, "A Machiavellian prince. You're young. You don't understand. But someday…"

"I'm young and in love with the revolution. *You* don't understand," I said, wiping away tears and adopting a defiant stance that *abuela* ignored.

As I reflect back on that moment, I wonder if *abuela* would have been as forceful about her instructions had she known the reality of what we were about to face. I understand my support of the revolution had lasted longer than it should have, but as *abuela* said I was young. And naiveté is the privilege of youth—believing in a magic act even after the child is shown how the trick is performed.

Next, *abuela* said, "We must follow the word of God if we want *His* rewards."

What was she implying? Was my going to Miami a punishment from God? As a devout Catholic, *abuela* said the rosary every day and attended mass regularly. I, on the other hand, had stopped going to church. Confessing the same sins every week ("impure thoughts") had become a tedious act. The fact was that once, after telling the priest about those impure thoughts, he asked me if I had ever been in love with a man. "No, no, no," I replied as stunned as if he had asked if I had ever killed anyone. That was my last time in church. This was even before Jorge Luís. The thought that I'd be discussing my secrets with a priest, or anyone for that matter, shook me up. Next thing I'd be talking about my participation in the looting of *abuelo's* stamp collection, and who knows what else. No, church was not for me.

But why was this a problem? I couldn't remember *papá* going to church, except for weddings, when he'd wear a striped, gray suit he had bought in Havana; or baptisms, particularly if he were one of the godparents. I actually could not recall him attending my own First Communion.

Abuela's next statement brought me back to the moment. "You can't tell anyone about the telegram. It could be dangerous, for you, your *papi*."

I asked her if *tía* Chuchi and *tía* Nena knew. They did. Both had ensconced themselves in their bedrooms. I assumed *tía* Chuchi had found one of her many jigsaw puzzles to work on—that's what she did to relieve stress, and she had assembled lots of them ever since she divorced two years before and moved in with *abuela*. A classical pianist, *tía* Chuchi had a Master's Degree in Music from the University of Santiago and often, as I practiced, shouted a correction from the bedroom. "No, not G flat. G natural. G natural."

Never married, *tía* Nena had taken to bed with her usual migraine. I remembered her always sick with a pain of some kind. Skeletally thin, she spent most days in her room, clad in a nightgown, usually a flannel one, despite Cuba's mild weather, with shutters closed and a bandana soaked in unguent or alcohol wrapped around her forehead. When she spoke, she would open one eye and look at you, her forehead all wrinkled, as if the world would come to an end if she opened the other eye. Occasionally, she would allow herself to consult the Ouija Board, particularly when *mamá* visited; these sessions, however, would make whatever ailed her worse and she would have to stop. *Very talented with the Ouija.* That's what everyone said about her. I never wanted *abuelo*, or anyone dead for that matter, to talk to me, so I stayed away from those sittings.

How I managed to convince the matriarch of the sugar plantation that I was going out I can't recall. Maybe I just left without telling her. I remember walking down marbles steps, covered in half-shadows since one of the bulbs on the ceiling fixture had burned out. The eerie darkness reminded me of the unresolved future I was facing.

After a few steps down the stairs, I met Nelia and her son, Joseíto. They were on their way up to see *la Doctora*, a jovial looking woman with soft, round cheeks—she never failed to send a cake for my birthday. *La Doctora* lived and had her medical practice in the apartment next to *abuela's*. Allegedly, *la Doctora* performed abortions during Batista's days for the elite of Santiago, most of them women from *Vista Alegre*—an affluent neighborhood near the *instituto* where I used to go to high school. Even *mamá* used *la Doctora's* services twice. I heard such intimacy during a chat she had in Antilla with her best friend Rosalba. "After four children, I couldn't deal with one more…my last procedure showed twins…imagine… they would have committed me!"

Nelia was a friend of *la Doctora's* niece and often came to visit. Joseíto, a boy of about three, was crying, his tears like a potent waterfall. He didn't want to go upstairs. He wanted to return to the zoo, a place he and his mother had just visited.

"Go Oren." That meant he wanted to go with me. Oren was what he called me since he couldn't say Loren, my nickname.

"He will take you to the zoo another time. He is going to play a concert now," Nelia said, her tone frustrated.

"No, no, Oren, Oren," he said. He pounded on the marble floor so hard, I was afraid he would break his leg. He grabbed my own leg and wouldn't let go.

I'm not sure how I was able to disentangle myself from these two, but somehow I hurried out and Joseíto's tantrum became fainter until it disappeared in the distance.

I wanted to replace my own inner tantrum with music. Mozart, anything. My insides stuttered:

Fa, fa, fa, fa...

No matter how much I tried, no music came out. An etude of silence took over. Even the activity at the bus stop across the street from *abuela*'s, normally frenetic, seemed still, a flat canvas with distorted contours, rather than a reality whose space I would enter.

But enter I did, and the canvas came to life; instead of a bus stop, a battlefield stretched out in front of me, and lifeless bodies touched my feet. Among the dead I counted many youths my age and younger who had fought in the mountains on behalf of a revolution I was supposed to betray now.

I thought of Joseíto. His world was the zoo. That's all he saw. The animals behind cages. His feeding them. I, on the other hand, walked through this battlefield in a joyless stupor. As I reached *Enramada*, a blurred Woolworth building to my right, in front of which was a juice stand where I used to get a *guarapo*, a drink made from the pulp of the sugar cane, I realized that the rhythm of my life had pulsated through these streets with exuberance and a blind belief in the future. Now everything seemed disjointed, lifeless. My world had changed. Death filled the air. I didn't know what it all meant or how I would cope.

As I watch my younger self lost in a labyrinth of streets he once knew so well, I want to wrap my arms around him in a comforting embrace. I want to say to the boy whose heart is breaking that I will never abandon him, that I will always be there for him and suffer in his place so he never has to. But, I can't. He has to learn to survive on his own. Children eventually do.

Chapter Five

WALKING AWAY from *abuela's* apartment, I wanted to keep on going until I reached the Sierra Maestra and disappeared into its foliage, hiding from *abuela, mamá* and *papá* the way Fidel's *guerrilleros* concealed their presence from Batista's men. I would have taken a million bites from mosquitoes rather than the venomous sting of a telegram. I would have even settled for a trip to the zoo with Joseito. But my mission was different from that of those rebels or of the little boy who flooded a lobby's marble with tears of disappointment. So, when I reached the corner of Heredia, I turned left and headed toward the *conservatorio*.

My mind dashed about like a race car driver around a track. A crash seemed imminent. I wondered how I'd approach the subject with Raúl. No Chopin or Mozart melody to embrace our interaction; no discussion of Arrau, Bolet, or any of the greats of the piano. Our conversation would have a different melody. Raúl had taught me how to turn a musical phrase into an eloquent sigh. I needed him now to find the music in the words of a telegram. I was determined not to go to Antilla, Havana, or Miami. I would stay in Santiago. And go to Prague. *He* had to help me.

The *conservatorio's* lobby was dark, typical of entrances to older colonial buildings. A fixture on the wall, however, provided enough light for Arnoldo to identify me from a few feet away. "Lorenzo, Lorenzo... the letter..."

"Raúl?" I asked.

"He went home for lunch...Let me get it."

"What?"

"The letter. Your scholarship to Prague...It just came."

"But, I thought..."

"Official," he nodded. "Even before your concert! I'll go get it."

He walked away, his eyes twinkling, his lips mouthing a made-up song, his hands shaking imaginary maracas. I rushed toward the back of the building and stood in the courtyard under the sun. Even the lizards had found refuge from the intense heat. Minutes later, Arnoldo came back and from a covered porch motioned for me. I stayed still.

Meanwhile, the last movement of Beethoven's Sonata, known as "The Tempest," poured down from one of the practice rooms; its *arpeggiated* melody grew in tension, paralleling my own. "Here, here," Arnoldo said, walking toward me. I wanted to tell him why I was there but decided against it. As director of the *conservatorio* since its founding, he was the revolution's twin. Could I trust him with the news? Would he hurt my family as *abuela* had predicted? I would take no chances. "Can't wait to tell Raúl," he said with a smile.

"*Gracias, gracias,* my parents will be so happy." My eyes felt moist. I took the letter and ran out, which I hoped he interpreted as excitement. Big spots of perspiration had settled under my arms.

As I left the *conservatorio*, I felt I was entering my own *Tempest*. Who was playing the sonata? In the past I would have gone upstairs to learn who the pianist was. Today I had a different agenda. I'd missed Raúl. Jorge Luís was my last hope.

My steps hurried me along the narrow, cobblestone streets. When I reached the corner of Heredia and San Pedro, *la catedral* stood to my left, an eclectic-looking structure rebuilt four times because of ransacking by pirates and devastation by hurricanes and earthquakes. On top of the building rose the statue of an angel. I made the sign of the cross—a reflex as much as an act of desperation. I remembered as a child asking about the Trinity. "How could God the Father, God the Son, and the Holy Spirit be one person?" "It's all about the faith," I was told. At the time I would set up rows of chairs in our dining room—my sisters would drape towels over their head for veils—and I'd play priest, distributing pieces of bread to simulate the host during communion. It was a time of innocence when the worst sin I thought about was touching the bread with your teeth. "You can't do that. You'll go to hell," I'd tell Betty and Tere, who never seemed to get it right. Beni had no problem. A perfect little Catholic, he was.

As I turned right, *Parque Céspedes,* a favorite meeting place for *Santiagueros,* was on my left. Its wrought-iron benches and weeping poplars *(álamos)* attracted visitors. Even with the sun ricocheting violently off the cement, a few people promenaded around the park. A few others sprouted here and there like plants in a garden. Some stood. Others sat. All engaged in conversation.

It was in that park that I'd sit with Jorge Luís, pointing at the *Ayuntamiento,* a building that stood on the north side of the park, and tell him I was a dot in the crowd on January 1st, 1959, when, from a balcony there Fidel proclaimed victory to a cheering mob below. *"Viva Fidel...viva Fidel";* it was in that park that I told Jorge Luís about my parents' efforts to send me to the United States, starting with the Guantánamo base fiasco and ending with *mamá's* visits to Sister Margarita, including the one I joined.

With a smile he'd reassure me. "Don't worry, we're not going to let you go. You're good for the revolution." He'd hold my hands then, a comforting gesture he adopted usually in a dark corner of the *parque*. An electrical current would circulate through my body, but I would ignore the feeling. His attention toward me, I told myself, concerned my career, my future. He was acting as a mentor, like Raúl did, nothing more.

As time passed, I started to wonder. But, I was here now not to discuss my feelings for him, but to say we had claimed victory too soon. Not only did I have a visa, but an exit telegram that had come from the revolution itself, the revolution that supposedly would not *let me go*.

I entered *La Casa de Cultura's* lobby, a sea of marble one could easily drown in, and took the stairs up to the second floor. The moment I saw Jorge Luís, I sensed something odd. His black hair, normally brushed backed in controlled waves, looked uncombed. His shirt showed wrinkles that seemed defiant, proud of their presence, as if they had just returned him from a victorious combat. He barely looked at me. I showed him the scholarship letter. No reaction. I told him about the telegram, his behavior still frosty. "Go, go," he said, fidgeting with papers that had piled up on his desk like a mini Sierra Maestra. "You don't belong here any more. Say *adiós*."

"But, I don't want to go," I said, looking him in the eye; those brown orbs, which in the past had offered me the wisdom of the world, now returned my gaze with a blank stare. "You said the revolution wouldn't let me..."

He stood up, partly obstructing the signed picture of Alicia Alonso as *Giselle* hanging on the wall.

"Say *adiós*," he said again.

My heart trembled. What could I say or do? "Politics change people so…" I remembered *papá* saying. "…turning mother against son, husband against wife, brother against brother."

It was as though Jorge Luís already knew about the telegram and wanted the goodbye to be as swift and painless as possible.

I thought of *mamá* and Josefa, how their friendship had changed, but I refused to accept the same for Jorge Luís and me. He was different. I'd shared so much with him. But it was too late now. I didn't belong here. Not any more.

As I walked away from *La Casa de Cultura*, I faced the *ayuntamiento* and stared at the balcony from which Fidel had addressed the nation that New Year's Day promising a different future for Cuba. Instead of his bearded face, I saw my own image on that balcony waving my scholarship letter at an imaginary crowd below. "Show me, show me the better Cuba. The Cuba Fidel had promised. The Cuba where I can be happy and my parents, too!"

The crowd responded with shouts of "Antilla, Antilla, Antilla." My trip seemed unavoidable.

Approximately two hours after the train left Santiago, a rich baritone voice announced, "Alto Cedro." The conductor lingered on the first syllable of the first word and spat out the rest. For accompaniment he had the wailing of a whistle and clanking of a bell, the strident music becoming softer and softer until its pianissimo hushed itself into silence and the train stopped. How many times had I heard him utter those words before? ¡Alto Cedro! ¡Alto Cedro! ¡Alto Cedro! His performance that day found me fiddling with my ticket, a beige piece of hard paper with brown borders and black letters that showed my final destination: Antilla, a small town that sparkled like a precious stone but had lost its luster for me.

Walterio, a man with a round black moon for a face, lived like my parents in Antilla. He up the hill, near *La Glorieta*, from which an aerial view of the town showed *el parque*, a narrow, concrete esplanade with poplars lining both sides, and Bahia de Nipe, a dark blue expanse of water where Catholic worshipers believed *La Virgen de la Caridad del Cobre* had appeared for the first time in the seventeen hundreds to two brothers and their slave. At the opposite end of *La Glorieta* and near the *Bahia*, my parents lived in a large concrete house that had previously belonged to my paternal grandparents; the structure looked like a starched white shirt plunked down on the south side of the street.

Walterio's alarm clock would go off an hour before his six o'clock in the morning train to Santiago; his shift would end on the return trip to Antilla. Because he knew me well, he realized something was wrong. "Not interested in a chicken sandwich today? *Calientico*. Still warm, like your mama's embrace." His tone was quizzical; his black and red conductor cap danced to the music of his words.

In Alto Cedro, I usually bought from vendors who peddled their goods from the platform something to soothe my sweet cravings: a *raspadura*, a dark brown concoction made of pure unrefined sugar, or a few *yemitas de coco*, a blend of eggs, coconut and sugar that looked like they had been brushed over with a coat of yellow paint. He had seen me engage in those transactions before and seemed surprised at my lack of interest today. Pointing to the window, which I kept closed, he said, "You'll never make it without something in that stomach."

His parental concern came unrequested. True that the length of our stop in Alto Cedro depended on our connection with the Havana train, whose arrival time was unpredictable—we might sit in those tired-looking leather seats for hours waiting for the moon to whistle our departure. Besides, we still had a few more stops to make, including Cueto, home to my maternal grandmother and aunt, a sleepy town where even the roosters refused to sing at dawn. But, my experiences in Santiago had produced feelings that hardly inspired a *raspadura* or *yemitas de huevo* moment, or cravings for one of Walterio's warm chicken sandwiches. I couldn't tell him a word. Not in Santiago, where we had started the trip, a city that sat in a seam of the Sierra Maestra, where Fidel fought his revolution; or in Alto Cedro, a place of sweetly inspired memories; and never in Antilla, our final stop. Although in that small town, neighbors knew your business even before you did. How long would it take before they figured out what I was about to do? And how will it affect my parents. *Abuela's* words resonated in my head, "You can't tell anyone about the telegram. It could be dangerous, for you, your *papi*." But did I have to tell anyone? The telegram was a government-issued document, and although it was sent to *abuela's* address in Santiago, who was to say someone, maybe even Jorge Luís, had not alerted the authorities in Antilla already?

We arrived in Antilla near midnight to find most of the town asleep, except for three or four men standing on the train's platform. Among them was *papá* in a white *guayabera*. His lips looked austere as if they had never smiled at his own silly jokes.

A few casual acquaintances disembarked and acknowledged *papá*. I wondered if they had figured out the reason for my trip. When Walterio descended and gave me a half smile, I was certain he knew.

I held back from showering *papá* with my anger. Instead, after the obligatory greeting, a kiss on the cheek, we embraced a voiceless duet. A conversation with him flowed with ease in a group; a one-on-one chat on the other hand usually felt as if I were performing a four-hand piano piece all by myself.

Timbita, so nicknamed because of a protruding *timba* (pot-belly) over a rather short frame, took my suitcase. He walked a respectful two-feet behind us. *Papá* and I took our mute steps up the hill, past the statue of José Martí to our right and the block-long *parque* to our left. As I looked at the poplars, *álamos* trees, a familiar music played in my mind. It was Joaquín Rodrigo's *De los álamos vengo, madre, de ver como los menea el aire* (From the poplars I come, mother, from seeing them blow in the wind). I'd heard Zoila perform this madrigal at *abuela's* apartment with *tía* Chuchi at the piano. The composition reminded me of the poplars of my childhood. I had strolled many times among them and enjoyed their elegant sway from Marielena's balcony while she, a high school classmate, and I studied for a history or math test.

Antilla, a town I had once found pedestrian, suddenly changed in my eyes. Once, I couldn't wait to leave it for Santiago; now, threatened with exile, the idea of leaving those gentle *álamos* crushed my backbone. In Rodrigo's madrigal, the *álamos* were from Sevilla. In mine they were from Antilla and part of my soul. Santiago's *Parque Céspedes* enjoyed a few poplars. The ones from Antilla were precious relics given to me since childhood for safe keeping.

Our steps continued to *calle* Miramar, where our house, next to an empty corner lot, awaited us.

I didn't know then that after that night I would never sleep on Miramar 47 again, that I would never get the alluring whiff of the ocean from my childhood bedroom window, or eat sandwiches for breakfast with fresh shrimps brought in from the harbor every morning. I had abandoned those treats when I left for Santiago. But I could always return to them. Now a different future awaited me.

How could Fidel allow these boys and girls—"our hope for the future"—to abandon the society he was expecting them to mold? With them gone who would keep the song of my poplars alive? Like Pamina in Mozart's *The Magic Flute*, whose father abducts her, our fathers intended to kidnap us. Unlike Pamina, whose mother, the Queen of the Night, fights to free her, our mothers participated in the exile plot. No Queen of the Night aria, with its signature F above high C, could rescue us from our misery.

We crossed the open porch from left to right. I recoiled at the tall Corinthian columns that lined its front; they reminded me of ghosts, the spirits of poplars there to haunt me. *Papá* pushed open the unlocked door and held it for me. I hesitated, unsure I wanted to enter. He thanked and paid Timbita. "*Gracias a usted, Don Lorenzo.*" Timbita walked away. *Papá* stood immobile for a few seconds and looked me in the eye. Could he feel the horror in my heart? Had he ever touched horror in his? Had he ever cried?

Damn telegram! Damn everybody! Damn, damn, damn! *De los álamos vengo, madre.*

Chapter Six

After Timbita left, *papá* brought my suitcase in. Without a word, he left Beni and me in the sitting room in front of one of the modern wall sconces *mamá* had installed to replace the antique ones that had belonged to *papá's* parents—*mamá* didn't like anything old.

"We got it, we got it," Beni said, waving his arms as if he were conducting an orchestra.

"What?"

"The telegram."

"The what?" I knew damn well what he was talking about.

"I'll spell it out for you. Havana." He did, and then continued, "That's tomorrow. Then, Miami." He started spelling it but paused midway, perhaps waiting for me to come in with a *cadenza*, an improvisatory-like solo passage that gives the soloist an opportunity to show off his brilliant technique. I declined the invitation.

Beni was wearing striped pajama pants and no shirt, a strange outfit for a conductor, but appropriate for stifling Cuban weather. I still had on the same shirt and pants I'd been wearing since morning.

He continued. "Talking in code…like a spy movie." He imitated *abuela*. "Loren is participating in a festival. I thought all of you should go. You and Violeta…Beni might want to join."

Of course they would talk in code. Who'd risk talking about an exit permit over the phone? Not when Antilla's operator was Belkis, who started rumors about Imelda's pregnancy, about Magdalena and Amparito, about Yara and the new doctor in town, who despite protruding teeth and bulging eyes, had no trouble being invited into a woman's bedroom, particularly if the husband was out of town. Belkis would never admit to eavesdropping. Instead, before spreading a rumor, she would say, "I have it from a good source." I was certain it would be a matter of time before she learned about the telegram and would tell everyone.

Unlike Beni, the rest of the house seemed still. *Papá* had disappeared, probably into the kitchen to get some water, a rare occurrence. Usually, he'd ask one of us to get it for him. My twin, Betty, and older sister, Tere, were asleep. A good thing, for the only person I wanted to talk to, anyway, was *mamá*. She owed me an explanation.

The door to the master bedroom was wide open. An invitation to enter without knocking. *Mamá* stood in front of a dark wood armoire; the bottom showed nicks left over from runs-in with a tricycle I rode around the house when I was about three or four. She was packing a suitcase, which lay open on the bed like a crocodile's mouth. It would snatch every piece of clothing from her hand even before she let go of it. Something in her eyes seemed different, as if she could see what was in front of her but also beyond. She avoided my eyes, perhaps so I couldn't see the pain she was packing into the suitcase.

"When did this happen…? Why didn't you tell me we had gotten visas and were waiting for the telegram?" I said without a kiss or hello first.

"*Mi vida*, promise you'll write every day."

"*Mamá*, I'm not writing, because I'm not going anywhere. I thought I was too old. Didn't Sister Margarita say… is she responsible for this?"

"No, no, she isn't…well, maybe. *Mi amor*, we didn't want to spoil anything for you. Sister Margarita gave us a name who gave us a name. Your *papi* had to see many people. And it was dangerous. We didn't know exactly when…when it would all happen. But you've known all along."

"And all along I said I wouldn't go. Told you many times. The revolution is doing many good things…and we have to sacrifice. It's doing many good things for me. Don't you understand?"

At that moment, my gaze fell on a small photograph sitting on *mamá's* vanity table: Beni and I dressed in *rumbero* costumes, white, ruffled, long-sleeve shirts with white trousers and red bandanas tied around our waists. Beni is around five, I seven or eight. It was *carnival* time. The picture had been there for a long time but as it is with things you see often, I had stopped noticing it. I figured *mamá* would want to keep it there now, so she could look at it every day and commiserate about sons who had left for a *foreign carnival* to which she had not been invited.

"You don't want to write to your *mamacita*?" The crocodile's mouth ate another piece of clothing. "Imagine how your *papi* and I will feel without you…your poor sisters too. Oh, they're going to miss you…and I'll…well…"

"How could you allow this? After José Antonio Alonso you didn't let me stay in Havana. And now…"

"You were too young."

"Beni's age. You didn't let me take the scholarship then. Now, you want me to give up my concert, it's in three weeks… and a scholarship to Prague? No, no, no!"

"*Mi vida*, you were too young to stay in Havana by yourself. Can't you see? You will write, yes?"

"No," I said, sitting on the bed and rumpling the bedspread crocheted by her mother, *abuela* Lola. Then, leaning over the suitcase, I tried to block her actions.

"Just a few lines, *mi cielo*," she said as she lifted my arms out of the way. "Manolo and Conchita will be at the airport."

What had happened to *mamá*, the person I could usually persuade to support me? She had convinced *papá* to let me live in Santiago to study with Raúl. I was her father's grandson, the *abuelo* who had left a music legacy I was supposed to live up to. How could she have erased my past and drawn up a new, unwelcome future for me?

"Imagine the adventures." She stopped as if to think what they might be. Then, perhaps not able to come up with anything, she said, "Make sure Beni goes to church. You know how he is about getting up in the morning." She looked at the open window. "Look, look at the beautiful moon. When you look at it, think of me, sitting here, looking at the same—"

"I hate the moon!"

"*Mi vida,* this is our only hope. We can't get out. You have to go first."

"Fidel is *our* only hope!"

At that moment, *mamá* retrieved from the armoire a pink linen outfit Claudina had made for her. Her expression changed. She became a coquettish girl, proudly showing off a new outfit, something one of my sisters might do. "Do you like it?" she asked, carefully shaping the dress over her body. "Lucila sent me the material." A beautiful woman, with a youthful figure and flawless complexion, *mamá* looked even more attractive now, the pink dress highlighting the blush on the cheeks that was missing when I entered the room. As she looked at her image in the mirror inside the armoire's door, I could feel the back of my skull burning.

"I'm not going anywhere. *¡Carajo!*" I said, jumping off the bed, as if touched by lightning. I took the scholarship letter from my pocket and waved it in the air. "Look, look, you know what this is?"

She ignored me. "You'll have a rainbow of opportunities..." she said as she folded the dress carefully.

"I have my own rainbow here," I growled in tuba-like fashion and grabbed the dress from her. I threw it on the floor. She offered no resistance. I planned to stomp on it when *papá's* voice stopped me in my tracks.

"Get that dress off the floor, immediately," he said from the doorway, his voice threatening.

"You get it off the floor," I told him.

"How dare you speak to me like that?"

"I'm tired of being told what to do." My voice broke "I've worked hard for my concert, the scholarship..." Then, after a big, gasping breath, I added. "You want me out of the country...because this is what fits into your plans...because this is what you...you...you want? You're not going to kill my dreams the way you and *mamá*..." I hesitated. *Papá's* figure grew in front of me, almost touching the bedroom's high ceiling. But I was not scared of the giant. My despair had grown an armor around me. "Why didn't you kill me too? Wouldn't that have been easier? *La Doctora* would have been happy to do it." I looked at *mamá*, and then addressed both, "I'll get out of here. I'll run away. I'll denounce you to the government. I...I should have never gotten on *ese tren de mierda.*"

I was at my most uncensored self when dad's hand slapped reality back into my senses. Childhood memories of *papá* spanking, and locking me in a dark pantry with threats of rats inside, flooded my mind. I started to cry as I crumbled the scholarship letter in my hand. I was that little boy again, locked in the pantry, begging to be let out.

"There shall be no tears. This is a moment of joy, a moment of joy." *Papá*'s voice flogged the room; in seconds, the tone became a modulated murmur. "*Algún día me darás las gracias.* Someday, you'll say thank you."

The light in *mamá's* green eyes had dulled. She had turned all feelings off. In fact, she had disappeared into her own shell.

I realized then I would have to say goodbye, to her, *papá*, my sisters, and to my belief that my dreams, my destiny belonged to me.

Beni was standing outside the bedroom door. My *coda* had finally put an end to his concerto. That pesky little insect! No, I was not going anywhere with him. Nothing would change my mind.

It was lunch time, the morning after my big explosion with my parents. We must have looked like the picture of a typical family enjoying a meal together. The father at the head of the table; the mother at the other end; on one side two sisters, close in age, usually dressed alike but not today; and opposite them, two brothers. Except that in a few hours, the nucleus of the group would change. One side of the table would be wiped out, erased by a political cause that divided the family. The anticipation of that moment created a silence that strangled us.

Growing up, the children hardly ate with *papá*, except perhaps for *Nochebuena* (Christmas Eve dinner). *Mamá* made sure we were finished with dinner and out of the way—in bed—by the time he got home from work.

One day all this changed and we ate together, watching the gradual collapse of our old chairs and table because of a termite infestation, and welcoming a sleek contemporary set *mamá* had chosen at one of *papá's* store. The new set looked like Formica. *Mamá* claimed it was painted to resemble the laminate.

We used our meals to share what had happened that day, from our experiences at school, to one of *papá's* encounters with an employee or one of his partners, to preparations for Carnival, to gossip about a neighbor ("Is Carmita really pregnant? Well, she's showing a bump and she and Roberto..."). Normally one voice would offer a joyful exposition, while another provided a perfect counterpoint.

Today, however, lunch was as solemn as a Requiem Mass; we could have been chanting, *Requiem aeternam dona eis, Domine*—Grant them eternal rest, O Lord.

The dead were on our plates: sardines. Food rationing had turned these herring-like fish into Cuba's faithful meal companions for the last few weeks. Because complaining about them was equal to criticizing Fidel, I usually pretended I was devouring a juicy steak, licking my fingers with delight. Today, I couldn't bring myself to say or do anything to disguise my feelings for these odious little creatures.

Beni broke the silence. "Sardines again...they are...are these leftovers from last night?"

"*Ay, mi vida,*" *mamá* said in mock exasperation as she helped herself from the platter. In the process, she spilled sardines on the white tablecloth. "*Mira lo que he hecho.* Look what I've done." She attempted to clean it up with her napkin.

"In America, you'll have ham steaks," *papá* said, after which silence sat back at our table again. All that could be heard was the clinking of forks and spoons, as intrusive a sound as that of feet scurrying to their seat minutes after mass had started.

A persistent knock on the door interrupted our quiet. "Are you expecting anyone?" *mamá* asked, addressing all. We shook our heads.

The uninvited guest was Arturo, our next-door neighbor, wearing a freshly washed and ironed, green-militia uniform

"Don't you want to join us?" *mamá* said as she removed the apron she was wearing.

"*No, gracias,* I'll be just a moment."

"We're celebrating Loren's concert. Come, Arturo, sit down, sit down. You know Loren's been offered a scholarship to Prague? We're so proud. Why don't you take a picture of us?"

"*Si, por supuesto,*" Arturo said but did not sit down.

Had she heard what I said the night before about the concert and the scholarship? She had ignored me then; now she was using all that to distract Arturo? Swiftly, from a cabinet that matched our new faux-Formica table top, she produced her old camera. The family historian, *mamá* recorded every family moment with pictures. No special dinner was allowed to start until she had taken photos of the table. This while we watched the food get cold. Then, of course, she would want photos of everyone. Because she insisted on taking the photos herself, she seldom appeared in any of them. I thought we had escaped all this nonsense today.

"Arturo, why are you here?" Beni asked. Not an unusual question. Arturo rarely visited us.

Mamá gulped. "Beni, go, go stand next to your brother. And you, Loren closer to your father. Just the two boys with their *papi* and me." Taking the camera from *mamá*, Arturo took the picture. "Now, now everybody. Tere, Betty, over here. You don't mind, Arturo, do you?" Then, without waiting for a response, but not before the group was just the way she wanted it and she herself had joined it, she added, "Everybody smile! And you too, Loren…after lunch you should go next door with Arturo and tell everyone about your scholarship…now, Arturo, now."

The camera had no flash, but I still winced when the shutter clicked.

Going with Arturo? I had no clue what had brought him over that day, but I remembered well what he had wanted from me long ago.

I was five years old and had gone next door to play with Renecito, Arturo's nephew. He was not home and a playful Arturo, who had recently married, asked me to join him in the bedroom for a game of "find the flashlight." As instructed, I went to find the hand-held device, allegedly in his pants pocket. The hardness that met me was not metal. It gave to the touch. I made a mad escape home.

I hid under my bed, using it as if it were a turtle's bony shell that would protect me from further harm. I finally came out to scrub my hands and cleanse them from any trace of Arturo's action. *Mamá* found me in the bathroom, still trembling. "What happened? Did you play with Renecito?" "No." "You look sick. Are you hurt?" "No." "Are you telling me everything?" "Yes." "Was anybody there? Arturo?" "I don't know."

Arturo's game stopped after that first time—maybe because of my negative reaction. Nevertheless, his abuse remained etched deep inside me, an experience I kept from others, until I shared the secret with an understanding Jorge Luís. "It wasn't your fault," he said. Years and a revolution later, it was hard to believe Arturo could look at me without a hint of guilt or remorse.

I wanted to say something in front of my parents and my siblings about the incident with Arturo. What did I have to lose? But then *mamá* asked Arturo to take another picture. Rather than obliging, he put the camera down on the table and said, addressing my father, "*Señor* Martínez, I'm here to take you to the station." *Papá* didn't blink. It was as if he had anticipated Arturo's intention.

The rest happened in a flash. *Mamá* pled with Arturo to take the friendship between our families into consideration—Arturo had actually worked for *papá* at one time.

"You can't take him away like that, Arturo, *por el amor de Dios!*" *mamá* said. "Not again." Beni disappeared from the room as soon as Arturo asked *papá* to accompany him. Tere and Betty joined *mamá's* hysteria with irrepressible tears of their own.

"It's nothing. Just a chat," Arturo said.

"*Es el comité. ¿Sí? ¿Otra vez el comité?* Is it the committee? Once again, the committee?" *mamá* asked. "And Reina, is she responsible?" *Mamá* was referring to the CDRs (Committees for the Defense of the Revolution) that had been formed on every block of every city to report counterrevolutionary activities. Reina, who lived across the street, was in charge of our block's CDR.

"They probably just saw *Señor* Martínez coming in with Lorencín late last night."

Oh, I hated that nickname. But, how could anyone have seen us? The whole town slept. Did they know about the telegram already?

In what seemed like no more than seconds later, Arturo held open the stained glass door that led to the main sitting room and waited for *papá*. Some of the stained-glass pieces were cracked—*mamá* claimed she couldn't get anyone to fix them.

I was not sure what to do. One thing was certain: *papá* and I had achieved some kind of détente; my anger at him had melted like ice over an open flame. Last night, in the midst of our argument, even during lunch, he had looked formidable, threatening, and I hated him, but now, a touch of vulnerability colored his face. I wanted to embrace him, to say I was sorry. *Don't take papá. Don't.* At that moment the one I hated was Jorge Luís, for keeping me blind to the ugly side of the revolution. But I also had contempt for myself. How could I have been so selfish and not see the reality now facing me?

    I ran out to the porch in time to see *papá* get into Arturo's car, an old four-door, brown Ford with a few dents on the front fender on the driver's side. If this were Santiago, Arturo would have honked several times before entering the busy choreography of incoming traffic. In Antilla, Arturo easily claimed his lane. As he sped off into the distance, I pushed my elbows against one of the porch's columns, almost etching its relief onto my skin. I could hear my insides screaming. It was a silent wail that reverberated in my stomach.

    In twenty-four hours, I had traveled a path that twisted in unimaginable ways: the telegram, the disastrous meeting with Jorge Luís, the screaming match with my parents, now Arturo. Where was it going to end? If I had denounced him when he first invited me to play the flashlight game, he wouldn't be around now for a diversion, political in nature, that threatened to unravel my whole family. Was his behavior condoned by the revolution? Was Fidel really the Machiavellian prince *abuela* had called him? Was Jorge Luís supporting a regime that was so callous? This road had dumped me into a river of questions that spiraled up to my knees.

    While *papá* was away, *mamá* took full command, bringing Tomás, another neighbor, into her confidence, and arranging for him to drive us (*mamá, papá,* Beni and me) to Havana that evening. Betty and Tere would remain in Antilla.

Around three o'clock that same afternoon, *papá* returned; his steps were slow and painful, his words hollow and few. "It was only a conversation," he said.

Despite his reticence to talk, his grief was palpable, turning on a switch of awareness inside me. In the decade preceding World War II, the Great Depression affected many countries around the world, including Cuba. During that time, a*buelo* was forced to close his business, and *papá,* a young man about my age, had gone to work to help the family. "It was my duty, my obligation," *papá* would say whenever he spoke about it.

It was my duty now to go with Beni to the United States; apply for visas for everyone; and get them out of harm's way. How I would do this, I had no idea. But…

It was my duty. My obligation.

I was in my room still wrestling with thoughts of leaving Cuba when *mamá* entered. It had been two hours since *papá* had returned home. A look of concern shot through her face. "You didn't touch anything there, did you?" she asked while pointing to my closet. "The green box."

"What green box?"

"I'm taking it to *Doña María.*"

"Arturo's mother?"

"She'll keep it while we're in Havana. They'll never check there."

Curious to find out what she was talking about, I opened my closet and way in the back found a twelve by twelve green box about five inches deep. I opened it. My jaw dropped, sweeping the floor in surprise: gold and silver watches, bracelets, necklaces, rings, several strands of pearls.

"Each *socio,* partner, took a box home."

"You're not supposed to do that."

"That's what we'll live on when they take the business."

"That's not going to happen. That's ridiculous. It's propaganda." The truth was I didn't believe my words any more.

"Go kiss your sisters. It's time."

"Amén," I said, as if answering a prayer. *Go with God. Amén. Kill your revolution. Amén. Kill your soul. Amén.*

I gave her the box back and went to the living room. I looked out the window and saw the car waiting for us. The evening had already sent the afternoon packing. Yet, the picture in front of me was as clear as the blue water *abuelo* and I had greeted many times on our morning walks when I was a boy. In minutes I would share that vehicle with a broken *papá,* a sad but determined *mamá,* an unaware Beni, a compliant neighbor, and my thoughts, which would range from duty and obligation to fear and puzzlement.

In Havana, we stayed at the Lincoln, a small hotel at the corner of Virtudes and Galiano. Beni and I shared a room next to *mamá* and *papá's.* I told Beni that in nineteen-fifty-eight, Juan Arturo Fangio, the greatest racing car driver of all times, was taken hostage at gunpoint from the hotel lobby. Fidel's *Movimiento 26 de Julio,* the group responsible for the kidnapping, wanted to stop Fangio from participating in a race sponsored by Batista's government. Fangio was released unharmed right after the race ended. Although Beni had no interest in hearing about Fangio, I force fed him the news to keep my mind diverted from the reality we faced.

We had often lodged at the Lincoln. Its proximity to *El Malecón,* the city's seaside promenade, and to Old and Central Havana made it a favorite with my parents—they were also friends with the owner. In the lobby, the marble floors, gilt mirrors and crystal chandeliers gave the place a European elegance that appealed to well-heeled ladies of Batista's Havana. I remembered them dressed in their imported clothes at the hotel's restaurant where they would spend hours gossiping over drinks and a meal. Those stylish ladies had vanished—had they all left the country?

When we went to the restaurant shortly after our arrival around nine in the morning, only Beni, my parents, and I were there. Our breakfast consisted of hot chocolate, made with water rather than milk, and day-old bread that stuck to our throats. "All that's available," the waiter said.

With prospects of a scholarship to Prague dashed and the absence of Jorge Luís to keep me focused only on what he wanted me to see, I could no longer turn my back on the breakfast scene. A revolution that found the arts important enough to deserve support could not provide the country with the most basic of staples: eggs, milk, flour? Fidel blamed the American embargo, which had started in 1961; the scarcity of food, and items such as soap and toilet paper, would increase as the years went by. When Cuba formed an alliance with Russia that was supposed to benefit the Cuban economy, not much changed. Cuba, known for its production of sugar and sugar-related products, exported most of its sugar supply to Russia, leaving little for internal consumption. Cubans with no sugar for their *café cubano*? That should have been enough for an internal revolt. Yet, despite the hardships Fidel put the country through, the revolution is still around, still oppressing those with opposing political views. When people ask me how Fidel has managed to survive all these years, I have no explanation.

The evening brought with it an invitation to spend our last night in Havana enjoying the sights; the request did not come with a "sorry, I cannot attend" response card. Nothing appealed any more, not even a walk through *Parque Central,* which *papá* suggested, a jaunt I had enjoyed in the past.

In a corner of the park sat a street artist, his work displayed on easels all around him. My parents insisted on stopping. The same artist had drawn their caricatures a year after my parents got married. Now Beni and I would have ours done, posing exactly as our parents had.

I gave my profile to the artist while staring at the statue of José Martí carved in Carrara marble—allegedly the first monument in honor of the Cuban patriot ever erected in the country. Some of his verses, particularly *La Rosa Blanca,* rest in my memory. I had recited the poem time and time again, despite booing and shoving from the big boys, at the foot of a much smaller statue that adorned the entrance to our *parque* in Antilla. On January 28, the anniversary of his birth, all schools public and private marched around town and ended up in front of his statue for a celebration with music, speeches and his poetry.

> *Cultivo una rosa blanca*
> *En julio como en enero*
> *Para el amigo sincero*
> *Que me da su mano franca.*
> *Y para el cruel que me arranca*
> *El corazón con que vivo*
> *Cardo ni ortiga cultivo*
> *Cultivo una rosa blanca.*

> (I grow a white rose
> In July as in January
> For the friend
> Who gives me his honest hand.

And for the person who is cruel
And breaks the heart that gives me life
I grow no thorns or resentment
I grow a white rose.)
—*Versos Sencillos* by José Martí

A white rose for Jorge Luis? Another for my parents? Another for all those boys who had bullied me over the years? I felt something cold travelling down my cheek, the side I tried to hide not only from the artist but the rest of the world. I looked past the statue at the Hotel Inglaterra, an edifice in the neo-classical style, whose twinkling lights flirted with the night like an enamored *señorita*. The building adjacent to it, the *Centro Gallego*, would be renamed years later, in 1985 to be exact, the *Gran Teatro de la Habana*, Great Theatre of Havana, at the initiative of Alicia Alonso. This building had enjoyed a historic past. Revered by artists and public alike, the place had vibrated with cheers and applause for the likes of Sarah Bernhardt and Enrico Caruso. I tried to engrave in my mind the contours of this neo-baroque building. I had attended performances there and realized I might never set foot in that theatre again and experience its magic. By then, I could no longer hide my tears.

Chapter Seven

THE FOLLOWING morning, when we entered the airport's terminal, exhaustion claimed our faces—no one had slept much. We huddled in a corner of the central corridor, our nostrils insulted by the odor of cigarette smoke, our ears pierced by the loud sobs of goodbyes. Women cried gallons and hugged children they were saying goodbye to. One woman, her face flat and red from sobbing, kept smoothing out a little girl's pink dress in between hoisting the girl up in the air and planting kisses on the girl's cheeks, eyebrows, and forehead. Each kiss made a popping sound. The little girl could not have been more than five years old.

A mural covering a large wall at the far end of the terminal had a strong declaration, "Say yes to the Revolution."

Then I heard, "Loren, don't forget to write to your *mamacita*. Every day, *mi vida. Me tienes que prometer*. Promise, please promise. And take care of Beni. Be good to each other," *mamá* said as she straightened my suit lapel. Annoyed at her fussing, I stepped back.

"Tica, don't worry," *papá* said. "They'll be back in no time. Fidel won't last. I tell you. In the blink of an eye."

"Ay, please, Lorenzo, *por favor*." *Mamá* forced a smile.

"I'm telling you." His words sounded false.

My eyes focused on the black-and-white pattern on the tile floor, a design of ragged lines that seemed to connect all of life's mysteries. If only I could travel on this road, alone, unraveling those secrets, receiving answers to my questions. What was I gaining by leaving? What would happen to my parents? My sisters? Shouldn't I stay now more than ever? Was I running away from my feelings for Jorge Luís? While I wrestled with these questions, Beni eyed everyone and everything with great curiosity and a smile that seemed glued on. *Do you know what we're about to do?*

"Please call Conchita and Monolo in case they're not at airport. I'm sure they'll be there. You have the number," *mamá* said, and then added, "Loren, *cuida tu reloj y el anillo de tu abuelo.* Your watch and *abuelo*'s ring."

Why would she think she had to remind me?

At moments, *mamá* seemed close to crying, yet the tears never materialized. It was as if some supernatural force stopped them. They came so close to the surface, you could almost touch them, taste them. Yet they would disappear inside an invisible well.

"We'll be together soon," *mamá* said almost in a whisper, now sounding a bit like *papá*.

Finally came time for our goodbyes. Kisses planted themselves on our cheeks (so many I lost count) and foreheads. Hugs tightened around us. The goodbyes were peppered with "please, please write" coming from *mamá* and "don't worry, we'll be together soon" from *papá*. The emotions exhausted us all. Beni and I started our walk toward *la pecera*, the fishbowl, a glass enclosure that separated travelers from their families.

"Can we get a ham-and-cheese sandwich in there?" Beni said.

"Don't be an ass," I said.

I looked back, throwing one last glance at the duo left behind. *Mamá* stood apart from the crowd as if in the center of a spotlight. Like a child who had been abandoned in the middle of the street, she looked vulnerable, desperate for someone to help her. In a pleading gesture, she extended her arms toward us. My heart softened *"It is O.K...it is O.K. We will be back in no time,"* I wanted to say. I took a step toward her, hesitated, turned around and walked away toward the unknown, a future that turned out to be much different from anything we imagined. "Goodbye, *mamá, adiós*, goodbye, *papá, adiós*," I said to myself.

Fear wrapped around my eyes like a blindfold. My steps faltered. Was this how people felt on their way to *el paredón?* Usually a firing squad is composed of three or more members ordered to shoot at the same time so no one knows who fired the lethal shot. My squad was smaller, more like an operatic duet, *papá's* baritone and *mamá's* soprano. But, I could feel their vocal rifles aiming at my back. Rat-a-tat. They fired. I was wounded.

At the door to *la pecera*, an airport official checked our passports and telegram. Her smile hinted she would rather travel to foreign shores than work the door. Right behind her, an officer who seemed to have relinquished all sleep in the past forty-eight hours directed us to a dressing room for a body search.

Then came time for our suitcases. Beni's passed inspection. The man who checked mine, a dark unkempt goatee adding to his unfriendly aura, counted each piece of clothing, taking pleasure in the process as if he were partaking of a mouth-watering meal. When he felt something inside one of the pairs of socks, his face turned sour. Investigating further, he discovered an extra pair *mamá* had put there without my knowledge.

"That's four. Three and the pair you have on." Since Cuban law allowed travelers to take only three changes of clothes, the officer threw the unauthorized pair over his shoulder onto a table where confiscated items were piling up.

"No. His feet get cold," Beni said.

Next, the man asked me for the gold wedding ban belonging to *abuelo*, a ring I had worn for months, and the gold watch my parents had given me on my last birthday. "That's *abuelo's*...and the watch ..." My voice broke. I remembered *mamá's* words. "Your watch and *abuelo's* ring. Take care of them." Did she have an inkling this might happen?

"They belong to the revolution. Get out of my sight," the man said, motioning for us to move on. *Adiós* to you too, *amigo*, I said under my breath as I watched him slide both ring and watch inside his shirt pocket. Belonging to the revolution? The revolution I'd defended so blindly? How many rings and watches can the revolution fit into your pocket? If my parents had left me wounded, this *cabrón* (bastard) provided the *coup de grâce* that ended it all. My heart stopped. I was dead!

The ring was always there when abuelo *offered me his hand as we walked down the hill and along the water on our way to el* muelle. *We would climb onto the pier and walk on the decaying wooden planks, avoiding the holes that would send us right into the water if we took no precaution. I was not quite five yet. We'd sit at the end of the long dock, our legs dangling over the pier, the blue sea of the bay extending for miles, way, way beyond what the eyes could see. Sometimes a few boats, looking as though they were made of paper, floated on the water. The small ones had fishermen in them. On occasion, a big commercial ship, with a black, rusty bottom and white top that looked like tiers on a wedding cake, would moor on a nearby dock. While sitting on the* muelle, *I would throw pebbles*

I had collected on our walk and watch them create a pattern of multicolor ripples when they hit the water. The bay, the world then belonged to abuelo *and me.*

As I walked to the plane, I knew this was not a simple walk to *el muelle* with *abuelo*. My mind grew wings, avoiding thoughts of the ring, my past, and I forced myself to land in worlds where my soul would find solace, where no one would talk of communism, where music, piano music (Mozart, Chopin, Granados), opera (Mozart, Puccini) would fill my ears with consonant, apolitical beauty that would speak not of *adiós* but of eternal presence. How clueless was I about the future I was facing? But, then how clueless had I been about the revolution? There was no turning back. Not now. All the goodbyes have been said, including one to *abuelo's* ring.

I remembered a big black caja, *a casket, the adults called it, in the center of our living room and many chairs placed along the perimeter of the room. Women dressed in black cried and fanned themselves with their* abanicos *to blow away the heat that interfered with their grief. I was supposed to be next door, but somehow I had managed to slip back into our house to witness the scene. I opened the shutters and looked through the iron filigree that covered our windows, echoing the lace mantillas some of the women wore. A line had formed behind the black car that carried the* caja, *and a sea of flowers, mostly white, covered the top of the car. A few people had gathered on the sidewalk on the opposite side of the street. Some would join the line that walked in mournful silence behind the car that carried* abuelo. *While they accompanied him on his final walk, in my mind I took his hand, a hand with the ring still on, and walked down the hill and over to the* muelle *to throw pebbles. When the pebbles made contact with the water, the ripples healed my loss. Our daily walks did not end on that gray, dusty morning when* they took him away. In my mind, we'd sit on that pier again and again for many mornings. Abuela *kept his ring.* "Someday it will be yours," *she said to me.*

On the plane, Beni took the window seat. There was nothing I wanted to see out there, anyway. No more goodbyes. Not to that sea of hands waving in the background at the departing passengers, or the land that soon would become but a dot underneath our soaring plane, a country I was betraying by my own weakness, leaving it to the mercy of those who perhaps loved her too much, and making her vulnerable to others who didn't. I'd said the last goodbye to the corpse of my past.

I had kissed Betty first. She looked me in the eye without uttering a word. As twins, we had a life of shared experiences and could read each other's minds, finish each other's sentences. Because she understood my feelings, there was no need to speak. Loyal Tere, on the other hand, said, "I will write you!"

The plane pushed through a blanket of clouds. After it had settled under a dome of blue sky, Beni said, "Your friend took your ring."

As I thought about the *ladrón* (thief) who had stolen *abuelo's* ring, guilt spread over me. I too was a thief. I had stolen from *abuelo*. In a locked cabinet in our dining room, *abuelo* had a valuable stamp collection, which, after his death, we kept for years. While I was in middle school, my classmate, Marielena, and I started to collect stamps and I helped myself to *abuelo's* collection to supplement what we had amassed.

By the time we returned the collection to *abuela*, I'm sure its value had been compromised. No one ever mentioned the missing stamps— maybe they weren't aware of it—and I never confessed to my truancy. At the time, I was trying to impress Marielena, wanting to be liked, accepted. Who else could provide access to such treasure. Looking back I wonder why the key to the cabinet was so easily accessible and why I was allowed, when *mamá* found me looking through those albums, to continue handling them.

"You're being careful with those stamps," she'd say.
"Of course."

Although the plane offered a smooth ride, Beni's words did not. "He took your ring," he said again. When I didn't answer, he changed the subject. "I think I'll have a cigarette." His eyebrows wiggled as he started to peel off the cellophane around the complimentary packet of cigarettes left on his seat.

"No, you won't"
"Why?"
"You can't," I said, grabbing the packet.
"You're nobody to tell me."
"Try your brother, for one? Older for two?"

While I tried to exert my older brother influence over him, I fretted. Would Beni still see me as a role model if he discovered about Jorge Luís? Or *abuelo's* stamps? I didn't have to worry long, for sweat settled on Beni's forehead while he sank deeper and deeper onto his seat.

With one forward thrust, he jerked the disposal paper bag from the back of the seat in front of him, and emptied his guts into it.

Temptation to smoke a cigarette myself flashed through my head. Seniority gave me permission. I ignored the allure and concentrated on the passengers who had turned the cabin into a political rally. "*¡Fidel, Fidel ya no te voy a* *ver!* Fidel, I'm not going to see you any more!" The chant grew into a conga line, weaving through the aisle until the pilot commanded everyone to return to their seats. After the conga ended, a heartfelt rendition of Cuba's national anthem shook our seats. Then, ignoring the pilot's instructions, a middle-aged man, with a moustache that covered his lips and blurred some of his words, stood up and recited Bonifacio Byrne's, *Mi Bandera* (My flag). *¿Dónde está mi bandera cubana, la bandera más bella que existe?* Where's my Cuban flag, the most beautiful flag in the world?

He had not finished his poem when a stewardess, her voice sweet but determined, addressed the passengers over the intercom. "We're preparing for landing. Please fasten your seatbelts and extinguish your cigarettes. I hope you've enjoyed our flight."

I closed my eyes. Only an hour ago, we were still in Cuba. In such a short time, I had left a whole world behind, my family, my music, Jorge Luís, a ring and a watch. The familiarity of it all I could still touch, caress. Why did it seem so remote then? As the seconds went by, the warmth of my past melted away until I could sense or remember nothing. An hour had become an eternity.

Beni squeezed my arm, a gesture I didn't acknowledge. I wanted to stop the plane from landing. Too late. It glided over the runway with the smoothness of a ballerina. I thought of Alicia Alonso. *You don't have to do a grand jeté. Just walk like a dancer.* The passengers burst into applause for two reasons: in appreciation of the pilot's flawless performance and because they had just landed in America. Many were paralyzed by their emotions and required help off the plane. After exiting, passengers kissed the ground in reverence, shouting, "America, land of freedom" "Viva America!" "*Abajo el Comunismo.*"

My mood was far from celebratory. For certain I was not kissing any soil. Arriving in America was one thing, but eating dirt was eating dirt.

Walking to the terminal, I caught a glimpse of the little girl with the pink dress being escorted by one of the stewardesses. A mask of confusion covered the little girl's face—later at immigration, I'd see her being handed over to some relatives while she cried non-stop, asking for her mother.

As we were about to enter the immigration area, I saw Beni take out from his pants pocket a piece of paper that looked familiar, stationery from the Lincoln Hotel. "Give me that!"

"I found it. It's mine now. Tell me, who's the girl?"

"None of your business." I grabbed the paper out of his hands.

"Tell me, tell me, who is it?"

I was in the habit of jotting down ideas, sometimes verses, as either poetry or lyrics to songs, and often threw them away. I had written this verse at the hotel and discarded it in the waste basket.

Say I can say
Adiós to Cuba
Land of mojito
And of Martí
But I can never say adiós
Adiós to our love
To you and me...

This picture was taken in 1960, two years
before I came to this country.

Papá circa 1942.

Mamá on her wedding day.

My elegant *abuelo* holding Tere.

The four siblings on the steps of Martí's statue.

Second Movement – Operación PedroPan Becas (Scholarships)

Chapter Eight

For many people, airports offer an irresistible allure. But, when you get stuck at immigration for more than five hours, an airport becomes a place that speaks not of exotic destinations to travel to, but a form of jail.

That's how Beni and I saw it.

Only after we heard someone was coming for us, did our faces find a smile and our mood turn playful.

"Who do you think it is?" I asked Beni.

"President Kennedy. Maybe Marilyn." With his hands Beni outlined a curvaceous figure.

Our game came to a halt when a different figure, that of a slender, tall man, slipped through the glass door and walked toward us. Beni and I looked at each other and gasped. "A priest!" we said in unison. I was not sure why we were so surprised. Except at the time, we knew nothing about *Operación Pedro Pan* and the Catholic Church's involvement in it.

Dressed in clergy's clothes, black pants and white collar, he was indeed our man. "I'm *Padre* Palá," he said. "Sorry you've been waiting so long. We weren't told anyone was coming in today. It's good to meet you, *muchachos. ¿Qué me cuentan de Fidel?* How's Fidel?"

After shaking hands, we followed him to baggage claim and waited for him in the exact corner he told us to stand.

Soon a whirlwind of activity wrapped around us. Passengers pushed us out of the way so they could retrieve their suitcases from the carrousel. The foreign sound of English coming at us from every direction added to our confusion. Minutes went by and he was still gone. I was certain he'd never come back. Would he leave us stranded here with no luggage, money, or place to go? As desperation was about to set in, I saw *Padre's* lips curved in an upward swing coming toward us.

He had our luggage, which we hadn't seen since Cuba and which he insisted on carrying himself. "Light as a feather," he said, lifting them, one on each side, as if they were barbells for exercise. "I guess you left Fidel everything." A feverish traffic of people entering and exiting the building interrupted our steps. Only a Spanish word or two reached our ears as we followed him to a station wagon he had parked in front of the terminal. By then, evening had turned on its colorful lights.

At the wheel, *Padre* had the poise of a pianist, which reminded me of Raúl, whose elegant bearing never faltered, even when tackling the most difficult pieces of the piano repertoire. I noticed gray hair crawling like little spiders above *Padre's* ears.

Every gesture about him was the epitome of aplomb: the way he looked in the rear or side mirrors, how he handled the wheel to turn this or that corner. He projected such confidence that for a moment I believed he would make everything all right. *As long as he didn't ask to hear my confession.* He talked about Matecumbe, a camp I'd heard about earlier from O'Malley and Jane, although they had been vague about details. "You'll be there with others like you," *Padre* said. "You'll make friends…and besides, it'll only be a short time." His words reminded me of *papá's*.

"So you knew to ask for George." *Padre* continued, "Well, here we are…"

I didn't understand. Who was this George? I wanted to ask; most of all, I wanted to ask about camp. What was it like? Why were we told they might have to separate us? Was that still a possibility? What about the other camps we had also heard about? The more questions that piled on in my head the more a blanket of silence covered me. Silence was for me a way of forgetting, of pushing away my fears. I learned that at a young age. If I was upset about a grade, or losing a competition, or bullied in the school yard, what did everyone say? "*Olvídate, mi vida, olvídate.* Forget it, don't talk about it. Ignore it." That's how I coped.

But ignoring the happenings of the last few days would have been as difficult as performing all thirty-two Beethoven's sonatas in one sitting. All that had taken placed seemed unreal. Like a dream. Dreams and life, life and dreams blending into one another and questioning each other's reality.

Calderón de la Barca in his play, *La Vida Es Sueño* (Life is a Dream), played with this uncertainty. His protagonist, Segismundo, struggled with the notion that reality was only a product of his imagination, and in the end he figured that everything he had experienced was just a dream.

I read the play, written in verse, in high school, and something I wrote for a paper then ran through my head as *Padre* continued driving.

> *Dreams, so quickly shatter when you say goodbye*
> *Dreams, some make you laugh, some make you cry*
> *Sometimes, you fly like a bird*
> *You touch the sky*
> *You own the world*
> *But there's no dreaming when you say goodbye.*

Those lines made me think of Jorge Luís; I winced. *Padre* must have noticed my discomfort. "No one comes here happy, but soon...before they know it...this is...well, they find joy again."

Olvídate.

We zigzagged through busy city streets as neon signs teased us with an American menu of opportunities: a Coppertone ad promising a fun time in the sun; billboards for cigarettes (with or without menthol); restaurant signs. So different from what I would see at home. These ads promoted wealth, personal fun I was unsure I wanted to claim. In Cuba, oversized posters would provoke, asking citizens to forget themselves, to sacrifice all for the revolution. I had accepted those messages because they were woven into the fabric of my life as a pianist—a life that was supported by a regime interested in the arts. "Endorsing the arts doesn't excuse the executions of all who oppose him," *papá* had often said, trying to warn me of the evil of Fidel's regime. "Once they take away your personal freedom, *olvídate*, nothing else matters."

Si, papá, olvídate. I was trying to forget. But how could I?

When *Padre* parked in front of an imposing looking mansion, he said, "A few boys are lucky enough to stay here with Monsignor. He's the father of the program...a visionary."

I had no idea he was referring to *Operación Pedro Pan*, an effort that brought thousands of Cuban children to the United States, and to Monsignor Walsh who had played a prominent role in those efforts.

Padre carried an envelope and handed it to the young man who answered the door. The boy, the "lucky boy," fourteen or fifteen years old at the most, was sporting an American crew cut, which I immediately hated. It was clear he and *Padre* knew each other, for after shaking hands they hugged. While I occasionally glanced at the boy who was blessed enough to call this place home, my eyes skipped to a red splash of bougainvillea that almost touched the front door a couple of houses over. It was planted in a terracotta pot too small for the weight of the shrub. I could smell the sweet aroma emanating from it, or maybe I was imagining it. Could you actually smell in a dream? Perhaps it was the thickness or size of the bush, or the lights directed at the bougainvillea that demanded attention. The vibrant color of the flowers reminded me of a red velvet cape I wore first in kindergarten playing a king in a play. *Mamá* made me wear it two or three years in a row. I was a king, a prince, a mouse, even a Martian, always donning that cape, and dodging ridicule from others. "You know how much love your *mami* put into making it? Look at the gold thread around the border. You can't wear it just once!" Finally a tear on the side retired it from my wardrobe.

When *Padre* returned, I was still wearing the cape in my mind, although I was unsure of my role in a dream that included a *Padre* handing an envelope to a Cuban boy, the fortunate boy living in a mansion, and Beni and me on our way to camp. Maybe like Segismundo from *La Vida es Sueño*, I was getting out of prison, coming to claim my rightful place as the son of the king. If so, should I go up to that boy and tell him that I belonged in that palace, that I was—

Olvídate, Lorenzo.

Any doubt about my obligation to save my family had disappeared after my conversation with *mamá* at the Lincoln Hotel. On our last night in Havana, after *papá* and Beni had gone to sleep, she and I went to the lobby and sat there, just the two of us, mother and son, sharing a couch and embracing a tearful goodbye. Our exchange did not include stories that I so loved hearing about her father. I wanted to understand the meaning of what was about to happen. Perhaps deep inside I expected her to tell me, it was all a big joke, that we could go back home and resume our lives. She in Antilla, I in Santiago preparing for a concert and a scholarship to Prague. I asked about *papá's* experience at the police station.

"They threatened to take over the business and wanted him to squeal on others, his own friends, his family" she said, looking down at the marble floor to hide her swollen eyes. Moved by the sadness of our moment, a few guests gave us concerned looks. "And if that were…." Her words trailed off. "This is the second time they've taken him…I'm sure it won't be… well, we didn't want to tell you."

"Why? Why didn't you?"

"*Ay, mi amor, mi amor.* They took Enrique prisoner the other day, and we couldn't go over and console Cachita. You can't show loyalty to anyone who opposes Fidel."

I squirmed. Enrique and Cachita were our neighbors and Cachita was Tere's godmother. If this had happened to them, it could happen to us, to *papá*. Next time it might not be just a *conversation* but jail time. No wonder *papá* looked wan when he returned home from the station. It was as if every pint of blood had drained from his face.

Right there in the lobby of the Lincoln Hotel, I decided I'd meet uncertainty and terror head on. I promised *mamá* I'd do all I could to get them out of Cuba. I wanted *papá* and the rest of the family safe. I even promised to write and keep a scrapbook of letters, postcards, and mementos to present to them when we came together as a family again.

Mamá told me then about the secretive network working tirelessly to facilitate the exodus of Cuban children to the United States—although she didn't know it yet by the name of *Operación Pedro Pan*. Through this elaborate web, composed of clergy and people involved in counter-revolutionary activities— few knew who the others were—Cuban children received the necessary documentation to enter the U. S., a Visa Waiver instead of a standard visa, and proof that they had been accepted to an American School, the latter a fictitious document. Fidel was being fooled, perhaps not, by the pretense these children were going abroad not as political exiles but to study. Even the dollars needed in Cuba to buy plane tickets materialized in the hands of parents whose children had received their visas; most of that money was raised from Cuban-American businesses in Miami.

Alicia Alonso's sister, the last link in *papá*'s chain of contacts, handed him the visas and airplane tickets for Beni and me. This news surprised me, but then I remembered *papá's* words about the revolution turning siblings against each other and children against their parents. Alicia, how could you allow the revolution to use you when your own sister was working to bring Fidel to his knees? At that moment, Alicia's grace disappeared behind the marching boots of a government just as corrupt as Batista's own. Although through *mamá* I learned who had provided my parents with the necessary documents, I was still puzzled. According to Sister Margarita I was not eligible for a visa. Not until I was in Miami for a while did I learn Father Walsh, he was not Monsignor yet, operating from Miami, had the power to grant visas himself to children my age. All he had to do was clear the names with the State Department.

As we left the city of Miami behind, I looked back to see the lights blur like watercolors into the night. In front, a landscape of darkness presented itself; only the moon's glow kept pace with our headlights. If only I were still that innocent boy who could get lost in a game of "trick the moon."

"You boys must be hungry," *Padre* said.

"Yes," Beni said, his voice tinged with despair.

"We'll get you something to eat as soon as we get to camp."

"We have to apply for our parents' visas," Beni said, much to my surprise.

"So, you're the talkative one," *Padre* said. "You can do that tomorrow."

Padre made a sharp right and the car crawled until it stopped in front of a wooden gate. "Someone didn't close it," he said, his tone sharp and accusatory. *Ah, he was human after all.* "No wonder it's beginning to collapse."

Behind the gate was a sign, which was hard to read in the dark. He pointed to it. "Matecumbe, Indian name." Then, he maneuvered the vehicle through the gate and down a dirt road, where a dimly lit log cabin rose in sea of darkness.

The light in the room was inadequate to see the forms we had to fill out. *Mierda, how many times do we have to do this?* "Just formality," *Padre* said in his now familiar tones.

What I wanted was the meal he had promised. My stomach squeaked like the faulty pedal on *tía* Clementina's piano in Cueto.

Padre motioned for us to sit at the large desk that dominated the back wall of what served as the cabin's main office. Several chairs randomly placed, and magazines strewn over the floor made the space feel crowded and unkempt. To the left was *Padre's* private quarters, which included a kitchen. To our right, two windows kept the outdoors out with curtains that came below the window sill.

"The dining room is closed now," *Padre* said from the kitchen. "You'll meet everyone tomorrow." A small chrome and Formica dining table could be seen through the open door. "I'm sure I can find something here for you. Can you see all right over there? We need to get a better light."

What we need is food. Hurry!

Beni took his jacket and tie off and placed them over the back of his chair. I didn't remove anything; I was as comfortable as I was going to be.

"I wonder what's out there," Beni said, pointing toward the windows.

"*Culebras, muchas culebras.* Lots of snakes," an effeminate-looking boy said as he burst into the room like an explosion of flour in Francisca's kitchen. Her ham *croquettes*, breaded, floured and slightly fried, left her kitchen looking as if ravaged by a cyclone. This tornado of a boy, wrapped in a white sheet, reminded me of her, not because he'd made an appetizing offer, but because of the same boundless energy I remembered in Francisca.

"Who's that?" *Padre* asked as he peeked into the room. Then, pointing at the intruder, he commanded, "You, Tonio, back to bed. You have a long trip tomorrow morning."

Holding the sheet tightly over what I assumed was his naked body, the boy asked, "One last, desperate plea? Please?"

"We don't keep boys here to grow roots," *Padre* said, disappearing once again into the kitchen. Although his voice was somewhat muffled by the sound of cabinet doors opening and closing and the clinking of glasses and plates, we could still make out every word. "Before, you complained all the time. 'They are doing this to me, they are doing that.' Now you want to stay?"

"Montana is…you know the stories. Montana is no better. Here at least I'm close to *mami*"

Why would this Tonio want stay in a place where he was terrorized rather than taking a chance on Montana?

"Don't let them send you to Montana or New York," he said in a whisper.

Why not, I wondered? New York was where Raúl had studied. In fact other than Prague, I would have enjoyed studying in a city I had heard so much about. The revolution, however, didn't like anything American. So while I was in Cuba all I could hope for was the *conservatorio,* and Prague.

"It's an orphanage in New York. Worse than death. Rodolfo escaped. Almost went to live with Monsignor, but no, he's here." Tonio took a breath and then said, "I want to wait for *mami* here. Unless you get a good *beca,* a scholarship, you're better off at camp."

What Tonio had done without realizing it was to explain the destiny of every one at Matecumbe, and the other camps, something I would hear more about in days to come. You stayed at camp until you were relocated somewhere in the United States, or your parents arrived, whichever came first. *Padre* had not mentioned any of this.

As he entered the room, holding a plate of food in each hand, *Padre* said to Tonio. "Out, out!"

"You haven't even introduced us, *Padre.* Where are you boys from?"

"Santiago," I said.

"Antilla," Beni said, looking at Tonio as if he had just been exposed to an infectious disease.

"Santiago? Antilla? Never admit it to anyone. Everyone here is from Havana," he said, winking at me and then at Beni. "And everybody owns at least half of it."

"Enough," *Padre* said, "I'll bring you boys some milk now."

Then as *Padre* moved papers to the side so he could place the food down, Beni and I looked at each other and gulped. "Sardines!" we said in unison.

Arranged in a perfectly straight line, the sardines twinkled like lights on a Christmas tree; next to them was a pile of saltine crackers. I felt nauseous. Minutes ago, I would have eaten anything, but the sight of these "former friends" now repulsed me.

"No more sardines," Beni said, pushing his plate away.

"Steaks, ham steaks, *papá* promised—" The unplanned words spurted out of my mouth.

Tonio's gaze traveled from me to Beni and back with an air of curiosity.

"Tonio," *Padre* said menacingly. "Tonio," *Padre* said again.

Realizing he had overextended his welcome, Tonio turned around. In the process, he dropped the sheet he'd held close to his body, revealing a well-toned dark back and white briefs—he was not naked after all. Without missing a beat, he picked up the sheet, covered himself up again and slammed the door behind him.

In minutes, so many dreams had shattered: ours for steaks or anything appetizing; Tonio's for staying at camp. My eyelids felt heavy; they closed as though they were an iron gate trying to keep trespassers out. The intruders were my own thoughts, and they had clawed my insides, leaving in their wake overall terror. What was this place really like? This camp where the feast that would placate our hunger never materialized; where a boy was often terrorized; where they sent campers to a fate worse than *death*. I stared at the dead sardines. And then I regretted the promise I had made to *mamá*. Why did I say I'd to anything within my power to help them get out of Cuba?

Dreams...so quickly shatter when you say goodbye.

Chapter Nine

AFTER BENI and I forced ourselves to eat some of the sardines, *Padre* guided us through a wooded path. The moon must have gone to bed for we could see nothing beyond the small light circle from *Padre's* flashlight. The rest was darkness, speaking to us in eerie noises; at one point a hissing interrupted our walk.

Beni's words spoke concern. "Are there snakes? That boy said…"

"Some," *Padre* said.

Then, as dry branches cried a soulful *danzón* under our shuffling feet, we heard a delicate tap, tap, tap, almost like a whisper; it was the sound of small feet walking behind us.

"Rats?" I asked.

"Well…" *Padre* never finished his sentence.

When we finally arrived at our destination, a log cabin similar to the one that served as the main office, except longer, I sighed. Ramón, who knew we were coming, welcomed us with the task of assembling our own cots for the night. His muscular physique made him look more like a professional weightlifter than counselor.

Padre promised us a real bed the following day, after the group scheduled for Montana left. "We're bursting at the seams."

Attempts at assembling the cots were awkward. *Where does this leg go? And that one?* We spoke in hushed tones. Campers were already asleep in rows of bunk beds that faced a center aisle where we were assembling our cots. Neither Ramón nor *Padre* helped. Our first test at self-reliance, at learning to survive in exile. Once we put the jigsaw puzzle together, Ramón went back to his own private room off to the side, *Padre* to his office, and we finally to sleep—or so we thought.

No sooner had Ramón disappeared than myriad miniature halos made an appearance, glowing in the dark like a chorus line of Tinkerbells. From those golden crowns, cigarette smoke danced through the room. A pillow fight broke out. A pillow landed on my face. I kept it.

The fingers of my right hand ached from clutching the handle of my suitcase to prevent campers from taking it; my entire body groaned from the hard cot. I thought I'd never fall asleep. But I did, and I dreamt about Tonio—maybe because I kept thinking about his willingness to endure the tormenting he was subjected to at camp to be close to his *mami*.

In the dream, we were in the bushes somewhere. I was asleep on the ground, still wearing my suit from Cuba and using my suitcase as pillow. The shuffle of feet next to me woke me up. Carrying a stick with a dead snake dangling from it, Tonio asked me to help him escape from Matecumbe. He was adamant about not going to Montana. "*Mami*'s in danger. They're going to kill her. I have to stay in Miami. She needs my help and I need yours." I knew all about making a promise to a mother, but why was he involving me in this?

I got up, grabbed my suitcase, and took a couple of steps away from him.

"Don't, don't. Please don't go. They are going to kill *mami*, help me, help me. Please."

At that moment his words became Beni's. I opened my eyes, not knowing for a moment where I was. Beni was running after a boy who had taken his suitcase. "Help!" He succeeded in getting it back.

It was then that I realized I had been dreaming; fear jabbed my insides. Was my dream really about Tonio and his *mami*, or about *papá*. An omen perhaps? Was he the one in danger of getting killed?

After breakfast, which consisted of an orgiastic (by Cuban standards) feast of toast, corn flakes, and hard boiled eggs that campers threw at each other outside the dining room, Beni and I trudged toward our new home—one of four tents set up only the day before and already looking like old ladies waiting to die. At least this was better than setting up quarters at immigration. Behind the tents, tall pine trees brushed the underarms of a blue sky. Our measly possessions jiggled inside suitcases made of cardboard that grew leaden with each step.

From my right, a boy of about sixteen approached. He wore khaki pants, and a wrinkled white t-shirt. His windswept hair covered one eye, an effect that seemed intentional.

He offered help with my suitcase. "*¿Te ayudo?* "

"*No, no, gracias,*" I said, looking at him with suspicion.

Then he addressed Beni. "*¿A ti?*"

Beni shook his head.

"I'm Miguel. Welcome to Matecumbe, *El Infierno Verde.*"

"Green Hell, eh?" *And is he the devil escorting us in?* I still expected him to try to snatch my suitcase.

Instead, he flashed a wide smile. "Which tent?"

"First one on the left," Beni said.

"Darío's. That's mine too."

Lucky us.

Miguel parted the opening flap and Beni and I sauntered in. Inside, on a wood floor, a center aisle divided rows of double-bunk beds that looked like pews in a church. Between the bunks, lockers stood vigil.

Giggles and screams punctuated the air, as boys claimed a bed and unburdened their belongings from suitcase to lockers, the way pirates empty their loot after a successful raid. We were all Cubans, different as we were. Our physical appearances reflected the ingredients of a *café con leche*. Some had coffee-colored skins. Others showed complexions as milky-white as the moon. Some had wavy hair; others brown oily locks that reminded me of wet sand. Our family configurations showed variances as well. A few whispered they came from divorced parents. *Scandal. Scandal.*

We also hailed from different provinces: some from Havana; Miguel from Santa Clara; Leonardo (my bunkmate) from Matanzas; Beni and I the only ones from Oriente. Cuba was our main link, but something else we had in common, the telegram. It was as if we shared the same beauty mark.

As I watched the smiling faces of these Cuban boys, little did I know that we were making political history and that one day we would proclaim with pride our participation in the exodus of Cuban children to this country. That we would say, "We were Pedro Pans."

After settling in, we headed to the main office to apply for our parents' visas. The pine trees that flanked the same path we had traveled the night before looked intimidating. Would we ever be happy here as *Padre* had promised? Again, I thought of Tonio. What was this place really like? What's going to happen to us? Are we, like Tonio, going to plead to remain here rather than venture into an unknown *beca?*

I had barely started on the visa application when a camper burst into the room. "*Padre, Padre,* Tonio is missing." The camper wore a gray flannel suit and a greenish gray tie.

Right behind him, another camper, also in suit and tie, flew into the room. "George is here, and he's going to leave without Tonio," he said.

Padre reassured them. "He won't leave without Tonio."

Putting a limp wrist to his forehead, the first camper mimicked Tonio, "Don't leave me, don't leave me. Wait for me, wait."

I wondered if my dream might give us a clue as to where Tonio was. *Mamá* believed in dreams, in séances, in talking to the dead. Would my dream tell us if Tonio was still in the bushes with a dead snake? I tried to remember what he wore. Was it a suit and tie like these campers were wearing, meaning he'd go with them, or the white sheet he had on when he barged into the main office last night? In that case, perhaps he was staying. No matter how hard I tried, nothing. I remembered the snake, his pleas for help, but little else.

George I remembered. My parents knew him and his family from Antilla. Eventually his parents moved to Havana, but the friendship with *mamá* and *papá* continued over the years. George had studied in the United States. Soon after Castro took over, his parents left Cuba, joining him here. It was a call to his parents that had saved Beni and me from spending any more time at immigration. I gave Jane the number, and she called them. They reached George, who in turn, communicated with *Padre* Palá. That was how *Padre* learned of our arrival. He mentioned this while Beni and I worked morosely on the plates of sardine. George's real name was Jorge Guarch. He worked for the Catholic

Welfare Bureau, receiving Cuban children at the airport and transporting them to the different camps. Many Cuban children, those who were not meeting relatives in Miami, had been told by their parents to ask for George the minute they arrived at the airport. His participation in a program that cared for unaccompanied Cuban children was known by many in Cuba, except, ironically, my parents. For us, having his parents' telephone number, however, was as good as asking for him. We were fortunate the piece of paper in my pocket with the phone number on it went unnoticed when airport personnel patted us down and later made us strip at the Havana airport. That *butterfly* saved us.

I asked *Padre* if I could go outside to meet George. Beni joined me.

In front of a large beige van, a handful of boys, travelers and well-wishers, exchanged pleasantries with a tall, serious-looking man. George's brows met in a frown, forming two parallel lines above his nose, his forehead extended far into his scalp. It was easy to discern the three or four travelers from the well-wishers; the travelers sported suits and ties, a sharp contrast to the wrinkled khakis and t-shirts the campers wore.

Making my way through the group, I introduced myself to George. He smiled politely then turned his back to ensure all the travelers were accounted for. I felt dismissed. A tinge of jealously swept over me. When *mamá* sang Beni a lullaby after he almost drowned, I thought the lullaby was mine alone, and because of my family's connection to George, I now had the same feeling about him. Nevertheless, share him I had to. George was a beloved figure, "a rescuer," to all the *Pedro Pan* children, and they never tired of fawning over him.

Padre came out to bid everyone farewell. "Did Tonio show up?" he asked George.

George shook his head. "His suitcase is in the van already. I have to go. We still have girls to pick up."

"Maybe he killed himself," a camper shouted from inside the van. "He couldn't take it any more." Then in a girlish tone, he added as if he were about to faint, "*Ay, ay, Dios mío, Dios mío!*"

In a strong voice, *Padre* addressed the travelers, "O.K., *muchachos*, onward. Good luck to each one of you. A new life awaits you. God bless you."

Then he said to George, "I'll take care of Tonio. I'll take him to the airport myself."

After the van had almost cleared the bend on the road, emptiness tightened around my throat. I could not imagine these boys going on to a *new life* when I hadn't yet made sense of my life here.

In the past, music had defined me, practicing, practicing every day, Saturdays and Sundays included. Perhaps I did it because of guilt, even fear. Once at age nine, I rebelled. Refusing to practice. I ran out of the house, dashing across the street, my eyes focusing on the path ahead. Then the impact. Something smashed against the right side of my body. A bicycle. Was it the fault of a distracted rider, or a careless, disobedient boy? An explosion went off inside me. Excruciating pain followed. Result: a broken leg and a cast I had to wear for months. "God punished you," *mamá* told me. Fearing another God-generated accident, I continued to practice.

When I turned fourteen, my love relationship with the piano was threatened once more. I was determined to quit. The reaction was triggered by my parents' refusal to let me stay in Havana, all expenses paid, to study, not the classics, but the popular music I had become interested in after hearing pianist/singer, Bola de Nieve, interpret his own Afro/Cuban compositions. The scholarship was the product of my being a finalist on the *José Antonio Alonso Program*, a popular television talent show. I placed second to a seven-year-old performing a precocious flamenco dance. My loss was sweetened by a special mention and scholarship, which my parents insisted I turn down. "You're too young to live in Havana by yourself," *mamá* said. That's when they let me move to Santiago to study with Raúl. Popular music, which I had enjoyed playing as a youngster, disappeared from my repertoire.

As I struggled to figure out what my life would be like at camp without music, I heard *Padre* say, "Go back inside…I need to go find Tonio."

No sooner had he spoken than from a distance down the path, a cloud of dust, propelled by a figure dressed in a dark suit, advanced towards us.

"Tonio," I said, pointing.

Padre nodded. It was the picture of a boy desperate to join the others. *Padre* motioned to a couple of boys to run and stop the van. They obeyed waving and screaming at a vehicle that deaf to their ruckus had continued on until it finally stopped.

"I was talking to Cuba…saying goodbye to *mami,*" a breathless Tonio said as he passed us by.

"Go, go," *Padre* told him.

"Enjoy your new life," I said more to myself than to him.

Chapter Ten

AFTER FINISHING the visas applications, we went to lunch. I sat near the end at one of three tables that ran the length of the room. Beni took a seat three places to my right; Leonardo, my bunkmate, sat across from me. From big bowls placed at strategic points along the tables, the day's fare teased our appetite: fried chicken, black beans and white rice. We had a new Cuban chef, hired to please the palate of boys who hated the American cuisine they had received before. Like the sacred host before communion, the food was off-limits until after the blessing. Multiple conversations blurred into each other, reverberating like Gregorian chant through a cathedral's hall.

Last night, I would have killed for this kind of feast. Now, sleep was the food I craved, seeing a pillow in every dish that met my eyes and a bed in every table top.

I waited for the blessing. A preparation for all the waiting we would have to do at camp: for our parents' visas, our relocation.

The shrill sound of a whistle shook the room. Through steam escaping from a bowl of black beans in front of me, I saw Darío, standing near the kitchen area. A young man in his late twenties with dark wavy hair and tanned complexion, Darío prayed: "Dear Lord, protect our families and dear ones in Cuba and bless this bountiful food which we are about to receive, Amen."

Echoing Dario's "Amen," the campers made the sign of the cross with forks in hand, finishing the ritual by stabbing a favorite piece of chicken. More than one fork landed on the same piece, which created a mild altercation. "I don't like thighs." "This breast is burnt." "I said I wanted that leg." At last there were compromises and exchanges of pieces.

"Better than sardines," Beni said.

Once disagreements were settled, the conversation turned to the dance at the girls' camp. I heard that any violation of camp's rules, including walking about after hours, swimming in the pool without a counselor in attendance, not getting up on time, not making the bed, and fighting would automatically disqualify someone from attending the dance, or getting the two-dollar weekly allowance campers received.

"You've not been here long enough," the boy next to me said. "No rules broken yet." He pointed to Leonardo, then to me. "You two twins?"

I could see the similarities: pale complexion, golden brown hair, eyes like a quiet sea *(abuela's* expression for anyone with light eyes; his leaned toward the blue while mine were green). Even our names sounded alike: Leonardo, Lorenzo.

"We only met this morning," Leonardo said.

I pointed to Beni. "That's my brother."

The same boy brought the conversation back to the dance. "Santiaguero, there are *chicas sabrosas* there. Maybe a *niña de Santiago?* You should go," he said with a devilish grin.

How did he know about Santiago? I hadn't mentioned anything. Maybe Beni had said something. "My name is Lorenzo," I said.

"*Sí*, Santiaguero…"

"My name is Lorenzo," I said, slamming my fork down. Why did he annoy me so?

"O.K., O.K," he said as he got up. Throwing his tall, rugged physique in my face, he continued, "I'm from Havana. You can call me Havanero." Then, he grabbed a half-eaten piece of chicken from his plate, dumped it on mine and said, "It's been a pleasure, *amigo*. We in Havana like to share with our friends."

"You little snake." I said, jumping up and turning my fists into boxer's gloves. I was about to throw him a punch when someone yanked the back of my suit jacket—I still had not changed into campers' wear, perhaps a statement that indicated my refusal to be of this place.

"You've been here less than a day. Don't ruin a perfectly good record," Darío said.

"He started it," I protested. My nostrils flared. I was not going to let anyone here bully me.

"I don't care who started it. Just be a good boy and sit down."

"*Una pelea, una pelea.* A fight," the boy seated next to Leonardo said. His mouth twisted into a grin of delight. Short and plump, he seemed to derive as much pleasure in my altercation with El Havanero as in the thigh he chomped on between words.

I pursed my lips and sat down. What I really wanted to do was punch the fucking Havanero, and Darío in the face. Here I was in a place I didn't want to be in, with food I didn't want, and hostility closing in on me. Fuck this camp. Fuck everyone. I was getting out of here. I looked at the plate in front of me and wanted to send it flying across the table. I could almost hear the big crash it would make as it hit the cement floor.

Leonardo must have read my mind, for he looked at me, and with a smile shook his head as if to say, "Don't you dare."

Two days later, Beni and I went back to the main office for a scheduled visit with a social worker. An American who had spent many years in Havana teaching English, Gary Jones had taken the job on a temporary basis as a favor to *Padre*. His white hair reflected experience, his soft smile sensibility rather than warmth. In my view, sensibility meant the ability to understand someone's emotion. And he showed that. Warmth, however, could only be expressed through affection, a real connection with someone's feelings. He couldn't give that much of himself to every boy who passed through his office.

He interviewed us separately. "Where do you want to go?" he asked me. Dario had asked the same question, so had Ramón, even *Padre*, after we had finished the visa applications. If you offered any suggestion, they would respond, "It all depends on what's available. We wait for a request for a particular number of children. Often these requests are age- and gender-specific, and although we try to keep siblings together, that's not always possible." I saw that as a threat. Keeping siblings together not possible?

What I didn't understand yet, was the complexity of a program that had grown way beyond what James Baker, former director of the Ruston Academy in Havana, had in mind when he approached Father Walsh, head of the Catholic Welfare Bureau in Miami, to help him bring children out of Cuba. After their meeting, they devised a plan and went to the U.S. government for financial support, which they received.

Initially, Baker believed they would be dealing with two hundred children, mostly children of teachers and parents from the Ruston Academy, most of them Catholics.

To keep the exodus of those children under the radar of the Cuban regime, Father Walsh worked with individual clergy in Cuba and some prominent figures of the counter-revolution rather than the official Church body in the country. His efforts evolved into the elaborate network *mamá* had mentioned that secured visas, sometimes passports, and airfare for children whose parents wanted to send them out of the country.

As the influx of new arrivals to the States continued—between 1960 and 1962, more than 14,000 had gone through the program—Walsh, who by then was ordained Monsignor, felt pressured to move the children out as soon as possible from a city that already had a large Cuban population. (Some stores started posting signs in their windows that read "English spoken here.") Monsignor reached out to Catholic dioceses and social service agencies across the country. Positive responses abounded, and although many children found refuge in private homes, some ended up in orphanages or reform schools where conditions were a far cry from what they experienced at home.

So, it was true that Matecumbe and the other camps depended on requests from different locations that were age-, number- and gender-specific. It was also true, as I'd soon learn, that we had no say in where we were sent, and that reversing a bad *beca* was next to impossible.

Despite all that, I said to Mr. Jones, "New York. That's where I want to go."

Two days after my confrontation with El Havanero, I sat after dinner on the concrete steps outside the dining room, trying to write home. I didn't know what to say. I remembered *mamá's* pleas, "Write to your *mamacita,* every day, *mi vida,* every day." Well, I'd not written since I got here.

A bare bulb over the door sent light dancing over the blank page that sat on my lap. Floating low in the sky, the moon's golden profile greeted me. I couldn't tell if it was a wink or an indifferent look. Was it offering *mamá* and my sisters, who might be looking at the same moon right now, a similar greeting?—I doubted *papá* would join them in the ritual. The moon connected us in a strange way. It was as if we were together in the same space though invisible to each other.

Occasionally the door behind me opened and one of the campers would go back to his cabin or tent. Then I would hear the ruckus of a Monopoly or Canasta game going on. The dining room became our meeting/recreation center at night. I was outside because I didn't want the loud voices, or even the silence of those writing home, words escaping from their pens in quick and fluid strokes, to distract me.

What could I say? I recalled our long day at the airport, our first night here and the dinner of sardines. My uneventful meeting with George/Jorge. Did they want to know any of that? It all seemed to matter and not at all. I refused to write about the desolation that came with the waiting game we had to play here. Did they want to know that we might end up in an orphanage? Probably not. But, should I prepare them for the likelihood?

I looked at the moon again. Please tell me what to say. Nothing. I stared straight ahead and noticed two eyes moving through the shadows toward me. In seconds they transformed themselves into the figure of El Havanero.

"What says the moon?" he asked, standing at the bottom of the steps. His voice was dark and textured.

"For one, that you're not invited to this party."

"I want to show you something!" he said.

"Not interested."

He grabbed me by the hand and pulled me down the steps. I scanned his face for a clue as to what was going on. Then without another word, he started to walk off. He expected me to follow, and without knowing why, I did. In synchronized rhythm, our steps shuffled through the sand and toward the path that connected the center of camp to the main office. He walked to my left. "What do you want to show me?" I asked. My yellow pad rattled in my hand, echoing my rapid heartbeat. He remained silent. I decided to turn back, but then, pulling on my left arm, he made a quick turn into the woods and took me with him.

I tried to yank away; his iron grip wouldn't let go. With his free arm he brushed branches away from our faces and scooted us into an area where the moon had set up a stage of pure magic.

Branches and bushes had been removed, revealing a clear, unobstructed circle of hard-packed earth. In the middle of the circle, a large rock of uneven texture reminded me of an altar. The moon peeked through the pine trees, settling gently at the end of the rock.

He sat cross-legged on the rock. "Sit!"

"Why?"

He smiled. "You ask too many questions."

"Why do you insist on bothering me?"

"I know you," he said.

I took a few steps, planning to retreat. "Please leave me alone."

"José Antonio Alonso? The young girl who stole first prize from you? The girl was my neighbor's daughter," he said. "I liked your playing. You should have won."

"I don't want to talk about José Antonio Alonso, about that girl, about..." I turned around, all of a sudden mystified "Why didn't you tell me?" My voice had softened somewhat.

"At first I wasn't sure it was you…but then…I knew. The boy who played *Fascination* was from Santiago. I tried to speak to you. I didn't know what you'd want to hear. You seem so angry…afraid… afraid of everything.:."

"I'm not. I'm not afraid of anything, and certainly not of you."

"Afraid to live?"

"No!" I almost spit the word out.

"Afraid to love?" His eyes searched my face.

My knees collapsed, touching the ground. Tears knocked at my throat; I refused to give them entry. Crouching close to me, he put an arm on my shoulder. "Tell me, what's the matter?" He whispered the words.

I could feel his breath warming my entire body. His lips brushed the left side of my face. I couldn't tell if this was intentional or not. "Let's get out of here," I said, pulling away from him. I attempted to get up but lost my balance. He steadied me.

"I'm leaving in a week…for Cincinnati, Ohio…and I wanted to be—"

"My friend?" I assumed that was what he wanted to say. "What if I don't want to be your friend? I'm tired of friends who betray you…of friends who believe a revolution is more important than…" My tone sounded disrespectful in a place that commanded religious reverence. I knew I was only masking my true feelings, for I longed to be touched by him, to feel the warmth of his body against mine and to lose myself in a physical intimacy that for a moment might heal the heartaches of the past few days. Maybe this was what I had wanted from Jorge Luís. Instead he had dismissed me. I had to get away from this boy now. A boy that weakened my determination. A boy I wanted to kiss.

"Let's go, let's go," I said, my voice quivering.

"I wanted to show you where we come when everything looks hopeless… enjoy Matecumbe. This *Infierno Verde* is like summer camp. Once you leave you don't know what you'll be facing."

Perhaps realizing my determination to get out of there, he led me by the hand, and we slipped out of the bushes. When we reclaimed the path that would take us back, we let go of each other. I wondered what I'd tell Leonardo. He was in the dining room writing home and I promised I'd find him when I finished my letter. The night's stillness engulfed El Havanero (I still didn't know his real name) and me. We were melodies in an art song that sang the mystery of our journey. Behind a veil of darkness, he entered his cabin. I couldn't explain what had just happened, except that as I continued walking toward my tent, the lento of my steps gave me peace.

Chapter Eleven

During the rest of his stay at Matecumbe, El Havanero and I circled around each other, keeping our distance, interacting only in front of others. A tacit agreement. Kind. Protective. It kept at bay the scorn that would short-circuit us if any semblance of intimacy between us would leak out. Not that anything had happened, but it didn't matter. Give these boys a hint of weakness, and they would turn into vicious dogs, ready to bury their teeth into their victims' flesh.

Tonio claimed he was terrorized by these boys because they had found him effeminate. He told the truth. At night while we waited for Darío to turn off the lights, campers would confirm the indignities they had inflicted on him, name-calling, spitting, shoving. ("*Oye, niña, mámame la pinga.*" Hey, girl, suck my dick.) And he still preferred this to Montana? This type of cruelty was part of *novatadas* (pranks). As a rule they were played on newcomers (although not necessarily). Tonio was not new to camp. A favorite prank was dumping a boy into the pool, clothes and all, with hands tied behind his back. At such a sight, my own breath would sink. Just when I thought the boy was about to drown, the campers who had thrown him in the water like discarded bait would fish him out. When these shenanigans were inflicted on an unsuspecting boy, no staff was nearby to stop them.

El Havanero and I did not want any of that. So, at lunch, to keep everyone unaware of our relationship, El Havanero's eyes would jiggle in their sockets, engaging me and everyone else around him in a game he didn't tire of playing. "I've ordered a special piece of chicken for you," he'd say.

"Only if it hails from the mountains of Santiago."

"A communist. Mario, Jorge, call the authorities. Deportation. Deportation!"

Laughter would rattle our plates and conversations would continue with El Havanero expertly guiding the exchanges as if he were chauffeuring a vehicle through rocky terrain.

Then came time to say goodbye.

On the day before his departure, a week after our moon encounter, El Havanero entered Darío's tent carrying a white and blue shirt rolled into a tight bundle, his body looking as if it had shrunk, his steps slow and unfocused. He had come to honor a custom well-ensconced in Matecumbe by the time of our arrival, information that belonged in a "Matecumbe Welcome Package," if only one existed. Before leaving for a *beca*, a boy would give to a friend a favorite piece of clothing he owned, shirt, pair of pants, swimming trunks.

The ritual confirmed enduring friendships. And for me, none more meaningful than the alliance formed with a boy who almost got me in trouble on my first day at Matecumbe and yet made me look at myself and the world around me with eyes of optimism—although I was still unsure how far I could take this new feeling.

"It should fit." His eyes wanted to say more; his lips didn't cooperate. Anxiety had etched lines on his forehead. At that moment, Leonardo scooted under the front flap of the tent and sauntered in. "What's that?"

"My new shirt."

"Where's mine?"

El Havanero canted his head but didn't answer.

His face mapped cities of concern. "I will write." A pause. Then he turned around and exited. Was he troubled by the thought of leaving Matecumbe? Of leaving me? Afraid of his placement in Cincinnati, Ohio? I should have rushed out, settled a comforting hand on his shoulder; told him all would be fine. I didn't. He had rescued my spirits from the bottom of despair yet I couldn't find a way to reciprocate? Was I afraid of what others would say? How I would be treated, if they saw me consoling a boy who had given our short friendship a dimension I still didn't comprehend? How could I be so cold-hearted? I knew how it felt to be abandoned by a special friend. Yet, as Jorge Luís had told me, I had in essence said to El Havanero, "Go, go. You don't belong here anymore."

Maybe I was afraid of opening wounds that would bleed and leave me too anemic to survive. Whatever the reason, I had treated him as just one more boy leaving Matecumbe. Many more would follow and new arrivals would replace those who left. This was the way of Matecumbe. Campers accepted the routine, and so had I, it seemed. The revolving door would turn and turn. We couldn't stop it midway. Part of our *duty and obligation* was to keep on passing through. To arrive at the other side without regret. No turning back.

My behavior still bothered me. I didn't like the new person I'd become.

Two and a half weeks after El Havanero left, I found a letter from him waiting on my bed. We had just returned from a Saturday trip to Miami. Instead of staying in the city, a group of us decided to walk to Miami Beach, where we bought hot dogs from a vendor who hailed from Cuba—he was a lawyer there. Afterwards we walked past dilapidated Art Deco hotels that protected leather-skinned retirees from further damage from the sun; before long we found ourselves in front of the Fontainebleau Hotel. Hearing that Sinatra was in the hotel, we entered. I remembered that in the late 40's, according to Jorge Luís, Sinatra had performed at *El Nacional* in Havana at a secret meeting of American underworld figures. Suddenly, there he was, his eyes the color of my blue shirt, the one El Havanero had given me. Surrounded by security men, all dressed in black, Sinatra moved toward the exit.

"Frank, Frank, look this way," a woman said as she tried to take a picture.

"Frank, here, here," another person yelled.

As I stared at El Havanero's letter, I thought of my day at the beach, which had been like a Chopin Impromptu, unstructured, extemporaneous. I had improvised with the vendor, with whom I spoke of Cuban performers, mostly Celia Cruz and Olga Guillot; meandered through the streets of Miami Beach; and modulated freely into an encounter with a celebrity. "See, I'm not afraid to live?" I said as I tore the envelope open, wanting to gulp its content all at once. I'd not gone past the letter's first paragraph when a guttural sound escaped from my throat, "Oh, no." I placed the letter on my bed, without releasing it, and leaned against the bunk. I could feel the hot dog I had consumed earlier, catsup and all, pushing its way up. My head swirled. My legs went numb. The room turned dark. "Oh, no," I echoed my earlier cry. His was a bad *beca*.

El Havanero was sent to an orphanage, and at night, as I tossed in bed and looked at other campers, most already asleep behind a choir of snores, I'd shudder. *Who else would end up in one of those unspeakable places?* El Havanero washed dishes and floors, and if his work was unsatisfactory he was beaten by one of the nuns and made to sleep on the cold floors. He had to fend off boys who carried knives and picked fights with him. Although he found respite in classes at the local high school, where he could interact with "normal youth," students eyed him with suspicion because of where he lived. "He's one of those thugs," they'd say. I had envisioned something better for him, for all of us. We had come here, some of us against our will, expecting to find a life of freedom, not one where our human rights were abused. Why wasn't someone looking into the problem? The complaints went to *Padre* Palá—I told him about El Havanero's plight—and Monsignor Walsh.

Not only were El Havanero's complaints ignored, but so were Tonio's suggestions that all was not well in Montana. Occasionally, a boy would escape from a place that had chained him to a miserable exile, and occasionally one of those boys would end up with Monsignor Walsh in St. Raphael. *A lucky boy.* A boy who would enjoy weekend excursions on Monsignor's yacht; a boy many at Matecumbe envied; a boy who must have been confessing his sins, otherwise his blessings would not have been so plentiful.

The fact was that the program had grown so large, and become so decentralized, the Catholic Welfare Bureau proved unable to track the children's living conditions once they left the camps in Florida.

Although at Matecumbe we were expected to keep a semblance of structure, in reality we were free to wander around at will. We would go to English classes—the program's attempt to prepare us for our relocation—given outdoors by a thirty-year-old widow, who dressed in black and white moved with the poise of a ballerina and the allure of a movie star. A magnetic smile colored her face—a smile that did not change whether it was disapproving because of a prank (campers would often bring dead snakes to class) or convivial. Margarita Oteiza, a former Ruston Academy instructor in Havana, became involved in the *Pedro Pan* program first as a volunteer, receiving, like George, children at the airport. Had she continued in this role, she might have been the person comforting us at the airport instead of Jane, and might have driven us to camp rather than *Padre*. But, she found the task, particularly of receiving the youngest children who cried tears of despair, too heart-wrenching. She took the job at Matecumbe instead, teaching English to boys who welcomed her presence but not her lessons. An intriguing detail about Oteiza was the heavy, oversized, silver man's watch that danced around her wrist. Boys claimed it belonged to her husband who had died at the hands of Fidel's army during Bay of Pigs, and that she had managed to retrieve it on a trip to Cuba as a journalist. Myth or reality? She admitted to the watch belonging to her husband, not to how she had obtained it.

Besides attending classes, we would swim in the pool; participate in physical education classes—which I seldom did; enjoy dances held every week at the girls' camp; go to Miami on Saturdays by bus, which would leave camp early in the morning and return in the late afternoon; buy candy and sodas from the canteen from our two dollar weekly allowance, and use some of that money to buy stamps for letters and cards to Cuba. Those who had friends or relatives in the city would often stay with them for the weekend. The conditions at camp were less than ideal—not enough bathrooms or showers to accommodate the three hundred children crowded into camp at peak times—so campers looked forward to their weekend escapades. On their return many would report on their conquests, which as a rule involved American girls; they stayed away from *Cubanitas*. "They won't let you fondle them."

Often, Beni and I made Saturday trips to George's parents or spent weekends with Carmen María (a second cousin of *papá's*) and her husband Rubén. Once a visit to them ended in disaster.

Carmen María and Rubén lived in Miami Beach on Collins Avenue, two blocks from the ocean, in a small, two-story, Art Deco pink building in need of some paint. They would pick us up on Saturdays at Bayfront Park where the bus regurgitated us, and we'd stay with them overnight. When we visited, I spent hours swimming and sunbathing, activities that were a substitute for practicing, and that I'd learned to enjoy since arriving in Miami. Carmen María tried to teach me how to play the accordion, an instrument she was proficient at ("You're a pianist...you'll learn quickly"). I so disliked the sound of that squeeze box—it reminded me of an asthmatic soprano struggling for air—that her efforts proved fruitless. The meals at their home were simple: rice and beans, cheese sandwiches, peanut butter and jelly, spam. The most memorable consisted of Carmen María's *Ropa Vieja* (Shredded Beef), which she served over white rice along with sweet plantains. She worked as a maid in a small Miami Beach hotel, her husband as a porter in a large Coconut Grove hotel.

After three months at Matecumbe, our visit that weekend would be a celebration of sorts. Our parents' and sisters' visas had arrived a few days before; I had already mailed them to Cuba. At last, *mamá's* unrelenting requests would stop, "*Mi vida*, see what's happening with our visas.

We're desperate." As if we had any control over the State Department!

The water sparkled like a diamond tiara, a different picture from the less than royal reality El Havanero and other *Pedro Pans* experienced in bad *becas*. A couple of hours later, Beni decided to go back. I, on the other hand, couldn't get unglued from what looked like the inspired work of an artist rather than nature. If ever there was a moment that helped me forget my distress being a refugee, this was it. But then water had held me in its spell ever since I used to walk to *el muelle* with *abuelo*.

By the time I went back to the apartment an hour or so later, my skin had baked to an orange color. I found Beni in the living room, pacing in front of the brown pull-out sofa he and I slept on when we visited. On the wall behind the sofa hung a print of Pierrot, the sad clown from the *Commedia dell'Arte*. Beni had borrowed the clown's melancholy and had turned it into a furious rage, teeth and fists clenched. "What's the matter?" I asked.

"He touched me. That *maricón* touched me."

"He what? What do you mean?"

"My penis, that's what." He became more agitated, sweat covering his forehead. "I'm getting out of here." He headed toward the door.

I stopped him. "Wait, wait."

"I don't feel well."

"You can't leave like that...not alone," I said. "We'll figure something out. Maybe we can call Darío. He'll take us back."

At that moment, the door unlocked and Carmen María, wearing a red sundress, came in. She was returning from the beauty parlor. Her short perm emphasized her approachable features: vibrant eyes and friendly smile. "*Hola muchachos ¿cómo la pasaron?*"

"Fine, fine..." I said, but my eyes must have expressed something different, which she seemed to notice.

"Are you O.K.?"

"*Si, si.* Well, no." I had to find a solution to the affront directed at Beni and indirectly at me. But how, how? What to do? What to say? "I'm not feeling well," I said. "The nurse, Sarita, I need to see her. She'll give me something."

"No, I'm not feeling well," Beni said. I'd hoped he'd keep quiet and let me get us out of this situation. Too late.

Carmen María looked confused. "Tell me what's wrong," she said. "I can help, maybe."

"We really should go," I said.

Then, from the bedroom, Rubén appeared, wearing shorts of a red that almost matched Carmen María's dress. "Did I hear you boys want to go back?" His face was the picture of calm. "What about the picnic later by the pool?"

"We can't stay." My words cut through the air like daggers. He remained impassive.

I remembered how confused I had been after the incident with Arturo. I was a little boy and didn't think I could tell anyone. If I had told *mamá*, what could she have done? Arturo said he'd accuse me of starting it. Would Rubén do the same with Beni? I didn't want to create a scene because of Carmen María, and *papá*. They were relatives, after all, and I didn't want Rubén, in an effort to protect himself, to blame Beni. I had to get us out of there and quickly.

When we arrived at the twenty-some acres of pines, I felt as though we would drown in its vastness. Soon, I knew we'd be rid of this *hijo de puta*.

Carmen María stayed in the car, a dilapidated old number they had bought from another Cuban, while Rubén went into the office to sign us back in. Beni and I waited outside. When Rubén strutted out, my fingers clawed his elbow. "Why, why?" I asked. "Why didn't you try it with me? You bastard!" Rubén gave me a "guilty as charged look," rushed to the car, opened the driver's door and got in. I didn't think Carmen María had heard my words, but she had certainly seen my confrontational attitude; a puzzled expression washed over her face.

Once they drove away, I caught up to Beni, who had gone ahead, and side by side we slithered along the winding path back to our tent.

"I'm going to bed," Beni said. "I'm not feeling well."

Before he entered, I asked him never to tell our parents. I was used to keeping secrets and to protect Carmen María and *papá*, I thought he should do the same. Without replying, he went in. I stood outside, caught in the stillness of an almost empty camp, since most of the boys were out for the weekend. The sun had lost its glimmering beauty. The splendor of Miami Beach's water had disappeared. I felt stumped. *Can you even trust family?*

Chapter Twelve

A MONTH later, as I walked toward the tent, I caught sight of a mattress, sheets, pillows, and camper's clothes thrown without regard for symmetry into a pile on the ground. From it, flames flickered like tongues from the devil. A choir of boys stared at the scene, hypnotized by the dancing flames. Above, a crimson-colored curtain covered the sky.

Who could have played such a prank? That's what it must be, a *novatada*?

"Meningitis," a camper, wearing a baseball cap, said. Because of the hat, I assumed he was one of Beni's friends—Beni spent every moment he could playing baseball at Matecumbe. "Ignacio has meningitis...*Padre* took him to the hospital."

Another camper said, "He can die."

I looked around in disbelief, unsure what to do. I didn't know what meningitis was. "Let's bring our mattresses in. We have to burn them...it's contagious," the camper with the baseball cap said, his booming voice as intense as the fire that raged at our feet.

Then, another voice, "No one is burning anything...This is all under control. Go back to your cabins." So said Darío. He was standing a few feet behind the boys who found it difficult to take their eyes off the bonfire. "I don't want to say it one more time. *Ahora...vamos.*"

Darío's words expressed the self-confidence that in him was as natural as rice and beans at a Cuban table. Everyone trusted him. If a camper had a problem, whether or not he was assigned to his tent, he went to Darío, who would find the right words to soothe the hurting soul. When *Padre* was out, Darío took over. If a counselor didn't know how to deal with a difficult camper, Darío came to the rescue.

While at camp, many boys would form deep bonds with counselors, teachers or other adults, using them as parental figures in the absence of their own parents. Sarita, the nurse had; Darío was no exception. He and Villareal (we always called him by his last name) had developed a strong relationship. Villareal followed Darío everywhere, and often when Darío drove to Miami to visit his aunts, he would give Villareal a lift into town. I wanted to be the one close to Darío. Many a night, my mind played tricks on me, wanting Darío to replace Jorge Luís, or El Havanero, and many a night I would go to sleep wanting a hug from him; instead, he would shout before turning off the lights: "Five minutes!" Darío, like Jorge Luís, was older than I. Both seemed to have answers I sought. Darío's had a spiritual undertone that, despite my rebelliousness at following the Church's teachings, comforted in a way that Jorge Luís' more pragmatic responses did not. Best of all, Darío's words did not try to convince me of the revolution's worth. At one point, I told Darío about my confused feelings for Jorge Luís, nothing about El Havanero. Rather than act "shocked" as I assumed my parents, friends, or even a priest, would, he asked what I planned to do about it. "That's not what I want."

"Feelings or thoughts without action are not sins," he said. A simple response. No judgment. His faith reflected the two years he had spent in a Catholic seminary in Havana before studying medicine for a year at the University. I was

still unsure God was so forgiving, but Darío's words soothed.
"Don't you want to confess to *Padre* Palá? Monsignor?"

"No, no, no," I said and he never pushed. No *Padre*, or Monsignor, in the world would absolve me from sins I was certain would send me straight to hell. I couldn't kneel in front of them and make myself vulnerable. Talking to Darío was different. He was not a priest. He was my friend. He could have been my Jorge Luís. In a way he was, when he reassured me I was not done with music. "I understand what you went through and why you're reluctant to play again. But you will. Give it time. It will happen."

Still in front of the fire, Dario repeated to the campers, "*Vamos*. Go!"

I had taken a few steps in the direction of our tent when Paco, a camper who was also staying in Dario's tent, approached me.

"What happened?" he asked.

"Meningitis."

"Beni?"

"No, no. Ignacio."

"Why is Beni in the infirmary then?" he asked, his thin frame almost translucent from the fire.

"What?"

"The infirmary," he said.

No point in continuing the conversation. I had to find out what had happened to Beni. A month earlier I would have blamed it on a reaction to the incident with Rubén, or too much sun, but I had no idea what to blame it on now. Did Beni have meningitis? How would I explain it to my parents? And if it was contagious, would I get it as well?

When I entered the infirmary, which used to be Darío's cabin, Sarita blocked my way. A short, plump woman whose almost white hair belied her age—she was only in her mid-forties—Sarita had a soft, yet direct manner that endeared her to campers.

"What are you doing here?" she asked, frowning.

"To see Beni."

"No, you're not. He has chicken pox and it's contagious, so get out."

"I had it. I had it as a child."

She was not persuaded. "I don't believe you. Go."

"I had it. *Sarita...un besito, ¿si?*" I gave her a kiss on the cheek, trying to break down her defenses.

"*Ay, este niño.* Go, go see your brother and leave right away. I give you five minutes, you hear? Five minutes. These boys need to rest."

Rows of bunk beds spanned the length of the room. On some beds, boys lay, some asleep, some awake and moaning. On one of the beds a few boys played cards. I found Beni on a lower bunk at the end of the corridor. Small, fluid-filled blisters had developed on his face and scalp. "It itches," he said when he saw me. "You think I'm going to die?"

"Not unless I grab you by the neck and stop your breathing."

"Would you bring me some comic books?"

"Comic books? I don't have any comic books."

"Paco... he has some."

"Go to sleep. Sarita says you need rest."

"I can't sleep."

"Then, write home. That'll entertain you...and will surprise them."

"Canasta!" a boy from a nearby bed shouted.

Later that evening, after getting into my pajamas, I approached Darío, who was putting something in his locker, and asked about Ignacio. He said Ignacio was being treated with antibiotics and would recover. At first I was not sure if he was giving me platitudes, but I had no reason to mistrust him, so I went to bed, relieved Beni and Ignacio were both fine.

Sometime in the middle of the night, I awoke to a hand shaking me. "Lorenzo, Lorenzo, a call from Cuba." It was Darío.

Inside a metal box attached to the outside of the infirmary's east wall was the public phone. During the day, a never-ending line formed in front of it—campers calling siblings at other camps—and although calls were supposed to be kept under ten minutes, most ignored the mandate.

"Hola," I said into the receiver, my voice puncturing the quiet of the night.

"*¿Mi vida, como están?* We got the visas. We're so happy." It was my mother. After a minute or so repeating the same thing, she said, "Your *papi* wants to say hello."

"*Loren, qué contento estamos. Pronto estaremos allá.* Soon, soon we'll be there. How's Beni? Where is he?"

I tried as best as I could to exhale my fears. "Well, he's... he's fine...sleeping."

"We never hear from him. Go get him." It was my mother again. She had taken the phone away from *papá*.

I didn't want to tell them Beni was sick. In fact, most of the news we reported to Cuba had a positive slant ("We're fine...everything is great. They treat us well here. We're having a good time.")—even letters from those in orphanages and reform schools hid the grim situation under which those *Pedro Pans* lived.

"The tent is far from here. We'll lose the call," I said.

"Why doesn't he write? Are you sure he's well?"

"He's well…really, really." A white lie. But, it wouldn't hurt them. "He says he has nothing to say. That's why he just signs his name to my letters." I didn't know why I said this; although it was true Beni had made the remark.

"*Ay, mi vida. Gracias a Dios que pronto los podré cuidar.* Soon I can be there taking care of you."

"Soon," I said my voice soft and trembling. I wondered what they'd have to endure here. *Papá* as a porter in a hotel? Or hot dog vendor? *Mamá* as a domestic? Beni and I would not qualify for assistance under the program for unaccompanied Cuban children the moment they arrived in Miami. My sisters would also be ineligible.

"*Besos,*" *mamá* said, and then, she put *papá* back on.

"Your sisters send you their love. They are in Santiago visiting *abuela,*" he said. "We'll join them after we get our monthly ration." At that time Cubans had a *libreta de abastecimiento* (Supplies booklet) that entitled each family to a certain amount of food and other basic supplies. Products included in the *libreta* varied according to age and gender. Children under seven years of age were given one liter of milk per day as were the elderly, the ill, and pregnant women. Adults over 65 received certain allowances as well. My parents had to claim their *ration* in Antilla; if they missed it, they'd get nothing. Although I didn't want them struggling in Cuba, I worried about what they'd encounter here. What was better?

After the call ended, darkness and fear, fear and darkness accompanied me back to the tent and my bunk. Thoughts of concern whirled in my head. When sleep finally came, tears marred my dreams.

Chapter Thirteen

WE WERE at lunch when I realized that our *adiós* to Matecumbe was imminent. Dario had walked over to me and whispered that Beni and I should report right away to the main office; I knew then. It had been five months since our arrival, and ours was on the long end of most campers' stay.

The anticipation of this moment had caused excitement ("The real start of your life in America," Dario had said, and part of me believed it) and trepidation (*How can I say goodbye again?*). Besides, what if we get a bad *beca* and end up in an orphanage?

Yet, for campers goodbyes were as unavoidable as bad food in the cafeteria. We knew that sooner or later we would be saying goodbye to one another. That was our destiny. No one could escape it (not even Tonio).

I had said goodbye to El Havanero, Leonardo (he had gone to Chicago to a good *beca*), and many others. As unaccompanied Cuban children, *"adiós"* held us together like stitches on a quilt; for years, one made by *abuela* adorned the bottom of my bed in Santiago. At Matecumbe, the squares in our quilt were the boys' faces, which would change faster than the making of a bed. By the time we had smiled a *"Bienvenido,"* we were saying, *"Adiós.* Write to me."

It was our turn to have our squares replaced, to leave behind the tents (the big building under construction where all the tents would be consolidated was still unfinished); the familiar ropes that kept these tents in place; the electric posts that provided light to camp and swayed as if to the beat of a conga drum whenever a strong tropical breeze whizzed through. It was time, after five months walking through sand that had captured our often rebellious footprints, to fly to the next phase of a program whose success, if success was defined by numbers of children served, was beyond anything its founders had envisioned. Lunch had become the preferred time to alert campers to their relocation. El Havanero heard then, so did Leonardo, as did many others. In the middle of lunch you were tapped on the shoulder and asked to report to the main office. You knew then.

Beni and I sat in the social worker's office. Acelio Requena, a *cubano* who had replaced Mr. Jones, greeted us with a nod and a bare hint of a smile. *Señor* Requena reminded me a bit of Mr. O'Malley, the immigration guy, not so much in looks, although both had receding hair, as in demeanor; both smoked. At least Requena didn't want to talk about *Bay of Pigs*.

"You boys are going to Pasco, Washington,"

The news iced the room. "Pasco, Washington?" Beni and I asked in a duet of surprise.

"With the President?" I asked.

"No, no, no...you boys need some geography lesson." His tone was condescending. He spun a globe that sat on a corner of his desk and when it stopped, he pointed to it. "State. Washington State. Here."

My jaw clenched. "No reform school?"

"No, nothing like that."

"That's like Canada, maybe Alaska," Beni said.

Señor Requena knitted his eyebrows and growled his response. "No, no, here." Again he pointed somewhere on the globe. "It is a good place." He encouraged Beni to find Pasco on the globe.

From his chair, Beni leaned forward. "It's not there," he said, throwing his arms up in frustration.

"In the Seattle, Spokane area. Pasco's too small. It's west. West."

Beni and I looked at each other. "You're sending us to Alaska. I'm not going," Beni said.

"It's west," I said using *Señor* Requena's own words. I truly didn't know where we were going.

Señor Requena couldn't hide his exasperation. "If you don't accept this, who knows how long it will be. Finding a family that would take two boys your age, it's—

Beni sprung from his chair.

I pulled him back by the elbow.

After Beni sat down, we nodded to everything *Señor* Requena said, which included the date of our departure, a week away. We signed our consent and then strolled back to the center of camp in what felt like a funeral march of sorts. Soon we would say goodbye to this road, the occasional dead snake, and the sound of dry branches and leaves crackling under our feet that we'd heard every day for the last five months: a symphony that greeted us for the first time the night *Padre* led the way and welcomed us to Matecumbe; music whose notes did not conform to any known key but eventually charmed our ears.

"Do we have to go to school there?" Beni asked in a quiet voice.

"Of course."

Then, mimicking *Padre*, he added in sermon-like tones, "We need to go to school, so when we go back, we're responsible, educated citizens that can shape the future of Cuba." He took a deep breath, held it for a couple of seconds, then released it in an explosive sound.

It was true that *Padre* had said something like that. So had Dario and others who worked at Matecumbe. According to them we had to return to a free Cuba as productive participants in a democracy that had eluded the country before and after Fidel.

"Why don't we just escape?" Beni said, more a proposal than a question.

Beni's ambivalence reminded me of my own stubbornness when I said no to the telegram. But, I still couldn't believe what was coming out of his mouth. We'd climbed on this horse, and its furious gallop would not let us dismount without consequences.

We would say goodbye to pines that had witnessed our kneeling in front of the statue of the Madonna to say the rosary, praying for our parents, for peace; hidden the likes of Tonio—in my dream; watched in horror many "initiation rites," or *novatadas*, and egg fights outside the dining room; served as backdrop to Oteiza's entrances to classes; heard secrets revealed in confession to *Padre*, sometimes to Dario; eavesdropped on arguments between brothers; and echoed the shouts from excited boys after a home run by one of the campers.

I will miss their trembling in the breeze, their perfect posture, their ability to be of the earth and of the sky. Goodbye, pine trees. *Adiós*!

September 12, 1962
Our *new life* in America began with a six-thirty in the morning departure from camp. At the airport we boarded

a Delta flight, taking off around nine o'clock and making a stop in Tampa. Most of us got off, except Beni, who was feeling airsick. A half hour later, we re-boarded and left for Chicago. According to a note I made on a Delta Airlines napkin, which I kept as part of my promise to *mamá* to maintain a scrapbook, "our lunch was delicious." *Mamá* had recently mentioned they were living on "Russian meat," an oily concoction that made sardines taste like precious caviar; I wished I could have shared my lunch with them.

From the air, what I saw of Chicago, the only other American city after Miami I had seen, I liked. Tall skyscrapers seemed to brush the underbelly of the aircraft as the plane descended. In Chicago we changed planes and airlines. Now on Northwest Airlines, we flew to Minneapolis. Based on what I overheard someone say, Minneapolis winters were brutal. The thought of cold made me shiver. I became airsick—Beni rejoiced at seeing it was my turn; to relieve my distress, a stewardess brought over a damp towel, which she placed on my forehead.

We changed planes again and at four-twenty in the afternoon, Minneapolis time, we headed toward Washington State, landing first in Spokane, the second largest city in the state after Seattle. From there, we proceeded southwest to Pasco. By the time we arrived, some fourteen hours after we left Miami, my body and mind felt as if they'd just come off a Jules-Verne-like adventure across the globe.

We had arrived in Pasco, thirty of us, to meet our new families. But a stay with family sometimes meant only a few days; later the children would be transferred to an institution. It had happened to many campers. What would be our fate? As we descended from the plane, flashbulbs blinded us, and a sea of microphones begged for answers our bewilderment couldn't provide. Articles in the local media about our arrival had echoed previous reports about the program. An article in the *Miami Herald* on March 19, 1962 had called it "the underground railway in the sky—Operation Peter Pan." A *New York Times* article on May 17, 1962 had used the same name.

"Are you happy about your trip?" asked one reporter.

Another asked, "Are you looking forward to your new family?"

"What does your family in Cuba think of your coming to Washington State? Have you talked to them recently?" someone asked.

"How does it feel to be part of the Peter Pan movement?" another reporter asked Beni.

"That's enough," a man with a buzz cut said to the reporters. "Anything these youngsters say could jeopardize the lives of their families in Cuba." He then led our group into a bus that transported us to our motel for the evening.

After dinner in the motel's dining room, we went to our room. The only people we had had any interaction with were the journalists and the tall man who had been at the airport waiting for us; his name was Heyward, or Hayworth, or Hardwood. I couldn't quite figure it out. He had a muscular physique and crew cut that added a military air to his persona and perhaps explained why he was treating us as his recruits.

"Tomorrow you will be meeting your new family," he said. "I want everyone dressed properly. I will wake you up in time for breakfast. Meanwhile, have a good night's sleep. No staying up. You must be fresh to greet your foster parents."

As I reflected on the journalists' queries, I realized that, even before they asked them, those questions had inhabited my thoughts, nagging, probing, demanding. Are we going to be happy here? How were our parents doing? How would I react to living away from camp without the support of others, *Padre*, Darío, Sarita, friends?

Would I play music again? Darío had said I would.

At Matecumbe, we were defined by the same constant: unaccompanied Cuban children waiting for our parents. We had each other for comfort. Here we would live with an American family, live an American life. Could we adjust? Would I ever see the other children on this flight after tonight? Some were youngsters I had known from Matecumbe. Others came from Kendall and Florida City, two camps also run by the Catholic Welfare; those were children I didn't know. Some, no more than seven or eight years of age, were coming with older siblings, who played parents to the younger ones. The responsibility of looking after Beni was already choking me. At camp, Cuba was an arm's away, but now the distance that separated us from the island had increased in its geographical and emotional abyss. This was Pasco, Washington, the opposite extreme of the United States. Beni was right. We might as well be in Canada, or Alaska.

From my bed I could see the neon sign outside: the name, *Ballerina Motel*, flashed across the top in cursive red letters. Under the name, a dancer, outlined in blue, kicked her leg up, up, up, then down, down, down. The sign brought back memories of Alicia Alonso. She of the exquisite, fluid movements. This one of hard, mechanical steps. Each dancer reflected a part of my life: Alicia, my artistic past, a past with a revolution and lies; the neon ballerina my new, unbending reality.

As I got up and walked over to the window, Beni said, startled.

"Who's that?"

"A thief. Go back to sleep."

I pulled the chord and closed the curtain on the ballerina's dance, which had failed to serve as a soothing lullaby. No applause for her tonight.

Chapter Fourteen

AFTER BREAKFAST, we lined up on the second-floor balcony to wait for our families. Visible from where we stood was the neon ballerina, still dancing in daylight. Terror gripped my insides. How could I divert this "adventure," our "new life," from turning into a bad *beca*?

We were in Pasco, one of three neighboring cities known as the Tri-Cities (Richland and Kennewick were the other two), all situated in a place where the Yakima, Snake and Columbia rivers converged. I found this out from a precocious little boy, blond and freckled, around seven years of age, who had accompanied his father to meet his new Cuban brother. When I mentioned the amount of dust being blown about, some of which landed in my eyes, someone told me, "This is a semi-arid climate, little rain and lots of sand." The dust reminded me of Matecumbe, except the sun here did not shine as brightly. Instead, a gray mist dressed the air. I avoided the gaze of those who came over to say hello, perhaps afraid of what I might see; *bad becas* swimming in their eyes like a school of sharks. My hand shook a bit more with each new person I greeted and each hour that passed.

Beni and I were the last ones to be picked up; by the time Mr. Tudor came for us, I felt so weedy I was afraid the local sand would blow me away.

Mr. Tudor wore a tie but no jacket. A man in his late forties, he had a weak chin and eyebrows that arched above dark-framed eyeglasses, giving him a look of constant puzzlement. "We're stopping at church first," he said. "To give thanks." I wasn't ready to give thanks yet, but what could I say?

The church lacked tall columns, murals depicting religious scenes, or statues I remembered in big churches or cathedrals in Cuba. A stained-glass window behind the altar provided the only color in an otherwise gloomy space. To the right of the pews, an empty, wooden confessional waited for someone to part its curtains and fill it with sins—certainly, not me.

We knelt, emulating Mr. Tudor's devotion with the bowing of our heads. My prayer was simple: "Oh, God, please don't let this be a bad *beca!*" Stealing a few side glances in Mr. Tudor's direction, I hoped to figure out what this man was like, what might be in store for us. His face remained an enigma.

On our way home, Mr. Tudor asked we call him dad (I couldn't), or Elmer (no way!). He told us we would meet his wife, Lois (our new mom), and our brothers, Mike and Jon, later. Lois was a kindergarten teacher. Mike was the same age as Beni, Jon two years younger; both were in school now. Since Mr. Tudor had to work—he sold insurance—he dropped us off in the living room and told us to make ourselves at home.

We explored the unfamiliar surroundings. In the master bedroom a picture of the Bleeding Heart of Jesus loomed large over the bed. The brothers' room displayed a few football trophies belonging to Mike and some watercolors signed by Jon. Neither the boys' room nor ours had bunk beds, a welcome change after Matecumbe. Curtains with a Western motif, saddles, cowboy hats and boots covered the only window in our room. I was not sure how this fit in with our Cuban background. It was a subtle message, I'd hear in blatant language later of our need to "assimilate."

The furniture everywhere seemed practical and unassuming, crowding every room, including the den, where a TV, washer and drier, and an ironing board competed for space.

Outside, off the den, a white fence enclosed a small yard. The grass, a faded green with brown patches in spots, seemed as though it had frozen overnight. It made crisp sounds under our feet. No flower bloomed anywhere. At one end a lonely, small tree struggled for survival, the only plant life around. Its sense of isolation reflected my own feelings. I wanted to hug the tree, to nurture it back to life, and in so doing perhaps breathe some life into my own.

Nearby, less than a block away, a tall metal structure rose next to a long white building from which a slender chimney spat out smoke mottled in gray and black. Like the smoke our lives felt dismal. We had found and explored our surroundings but would we ever find the *family* living here?

For dinner that night we had mashed potatoes and gravy, pot roast, corn, celery sticks, and Jell-O for dessert. Although the food looked familiar, the flavors—duller than those at a Cuban table—hardly awakened the palate.

The spitfire speed of the conversation made it difficult for us with our limited vocabulary to understand all that was being said—I should have taken Oteiza's lessons more seriously. Mrs. Tudor kept talking about her class and one student in particular. "She's a real character," she said several times. Mr. Tudor did not mention his work. Whatever else he said escaped us. His eyes scanned the table time and time again, in what looked like a desperate attempt to understand his family's new composition.

Like the father, the brothers had weak chins. The older boy was tall and muscular. The younger, about Beni's height, displayed bloated cheeks like a chipmunk.

I recalled our last meal in Antilla when Arturo's visit interrupted us. How I wished I could go back to that room with people I loved, with the breeze from the bay coming in, even if I were eating sardines and fighting with my family about Fidel's revolution; my eyes would have opened eventually. Instead, I was having mashed potatoes and roast in a place that was suffocating me and chilled my insides at the same time.

Although we didn't hear anything about it that night, next day we were given our "chores." Beni and I would alternate "dishes duties" with Mike and Jon; Mike would take the garbage out every night. We were also responsible for preparing our own lunch—if we forgot to make it, we wouldn't eat. The Tudors would not give us "money to buy lunch in the school cafeteria." The days of having our meals taken care of by a cook at Matecumbe or Francisca or *mamá* were over.

The vacuuming chore fell to Beni and me, which we were supposed to do every weekend. The first Saturday the Tudors handed us the vacuum cleaner while they went to the store, neither Beni nor I had any idea how to operate that monster. In Cuba, floors are tiled rather than carpeted and they are swept and washed, not vacuumed. After a few feeble attempts that reminded me of our first night in Matecumbe setting up our cots, we figured out how to work the strange contraption. "This is something from Mars," I remembered saying.

When dinner came to an end, I felt as though I'd given two piano recitals back to back. All energy had drained from me. No one in the family spoke a word of Spanish, except "*Hola amigo,*" which the older brother said many times, accompanied by a jerky smile that didn't feel genuine.

Beni and I couldn't wait to jump into bed. We wore flannel pajamas the Tudors had bought for us in a Western print that matched our window curtains. Mr. Tudor stood at the door and led us in prayer. When we finished, he turned the light off and closed the door behind him. *Please God, don't let me dream of Tonio and his mami getting killed, or of papá's facing the revolution's wrath. But thank you… thank you for not sending us to an orphanage.*

The Tudors' home was in Kennewick, south of the Colombia River, rather than Pasco, where initially I thought it might be; no one from our group had been assigned to Pasco. Two siblings, boy and girl, ended up in Richland. The other *Pedro Pans* had been scattered throughout the different counties that made up the Tri-Cities. Some children went to live in farms. No one had ended up in orphanages.

Chapter Fifteen

A MONTH after our arrival, our *Pedro Pan* group was having a get-together in Richland—Mr. and Mrs. Peterson had read about us in the *Tri-Cities Herald*, the local newspaper, and had decided to host a party in our honor. Because we were in separate neighboring towns, up to then the group's only contact had been by phone. There had been no celebration, and oh, did we need one. Besides attending school, all Beni and I seemed to do was go to church. Not that going to church was all drudgery. In fact, the first time we went to confession we became players in a comedy skit that delighted us no end.

The priest had created a list of questions, which he had translated into Spanish, and had insisted on using it on Beni and me together. Somehow, a double confession made the ritual less intimidating. I felt I was play acting—I could have used the red cape *mamá* had made for me.

We knelt in front of the priest, no curtain hiding our awkwardness. "Have you had any unchristian thoughts?" he said in a hard to recognize Spanish. "Yes," we said." "How many?" "Three," I said. "Five," Beni responded. I didn't know how he kept track of who was saying what. Then came the spicy question. "Have you had any *acción de carne?*" He had translated carnal experience literally into "meat action."

I knew what he meant as did Beni. But, he, not one to let the possibility of a joke slip by, said, "You mean like lunchmeat?" When the priest didn't respond, Beni answered his own question. "Well no, we only get peanut butter and jelly sandwiches."

At that moment, laughter came out of us in uncontrollable jerks and we left the confessionary holding onto our convulsing bellies. When we regained our composure, we returned to face a priest who seemed bewildered and unsure how to proceed; his facial features had darkened.

Even after we became more proficient in the English language and had individual confessions, mine were intended to appease the Tudors. I was condemned to hell already, so it didn't matter. I would come up with a few made up sins, nothing about Jorge Luís, El Havanero, or even the Tudors, and after absolution, I'd take communion to the delight of our devout Catholic family. Confessing in a language foreign to us had made it less personal, providing a distance that allowed me to talk about my sins as if someone else had committed them.

The gathering of local *Pedro Pans* would cement our bond as unaccompanied Cuban children, and, I hoped, ease our anxiety over accounts that Russian missiles were propagating in Cuba. Everyone spoke of a possible nuclear war, which would mean not only the end of exit visas for our parents but the end of life itself. We needed distraction as our minds wrestled with fear; no calls to Cuba were possible to confirm or dispel the rumors about the missiles.

The Tudors claimed it was all propaganda to instill anxiety in all of us. But, the night before our party, President Kennedy, in a televised radio speech, announced the discovery of the missiles. There you go, Mom and Dad Tudor! *Propaganda, eh?*

> *"It shall be the policy of this nation to regard any nuclear missile launched from Cuba against any nation in the Western hemisphere as an attack on the United States, requiring a full retaliatory response upon the Soviet Union."*
> J. F. Kennedy, October 15, 1962

Mr. Tudor drove us over to Richland and promised to bring his wife over later—the brothers had not joined us. Because Mrs. Peterson used the basement where the party was held to teach dance, ballet *barres* and wall mirrors dominated the visuals. Reflected on the mirrors were our Cuban friends and members of their new families. An animated Glorita, one of the Cuban girls, rushed in one direction toward a girl she knew, kissed her on the cheeks, and glided to the other side, waving her arms. There she kissed one of the young boys on the head. When she saw me, she sprinted over and introduced me to Maggie, a 15 year-old cellist, blonde and petite, whom she had just met. Maggie was a friend of the Petersons' daughters. Because Glorita knew I played the piano, she insisted Maggie and I play something—Maggie had not brought her cello. Glorita pointed to a piano pushed to a corner of the room, and my curiosity led me to it, an upright Knabe with beautifully carved legs in the Victorian style.

With one finger, I played a few notes, eliciting an out-of-tune cry from the instrument. Yet I sat down, partly because I was egged on by many, including Mrs. Peterson, and partly because after not having touched a piano for six months, I wondered how it would feel. I played the first movement of Haydn's Sonata in F minor. With the exception of Mrs. Peterson, the reception was lukewarm. No surprise. My technique had gone into exile, leaving behind only a shadow of what it once was. Playing the piano, however, felt as though

I were meeting a long lost friend, although anxious sweat danced through my fingers. None of the Cuban boys and girls wanted more classical pieces. "Play *Autumn Leaves*," someone said. It seemed they'd already Americanized their musical taste. Because I couldn't oblige them—I had not played popular music since my performance on the José Antonio Alonso program—I chose Lecuona's *Malagueña*. When I finished, rusty technique and an out-of-tune instrument notwithstanding, loud applause echoed through the room, led by Mrs. Peterson, who was curious as to my plans to resume my musical studies here. For a few moments all thoughts of nuclear war went into hiding, replaced by the warmth these boys, girls and adults showered upon me. Cuba seemed so far away. Russia too. Communism had been obliterated from my eyes.

I didn't mention to Mrs. Peterson the Tudors had no piano. When a somber looking Mr. Tudor arrived without his wife, Mrs. Peterson insisted they nurture my musical talents. "You should have heard….you should have heard how he played!" Mrs. Peterson would remain a supporter and trusted friend during my stay in Kennewick and beyond.

On our way home, Mr. Tudor had more things on his mind than my music. By then my worries about my parents and the blockade had returned. Mr. Tudor explained, recitative-like, Mike had gotten into trouble and the police had been involved. It was something about a "joy ride," an expression that took me a while to understand. He had been babysitting at a neighbor's, taken their car and gone for a ride. "Underage, no license, stolen car, no good," he kept saying. Since I was seated in the passenger seat, occasionally he would wave a finger at me as if to warn me not to try anything similar.

With the party over, we were back to our daily reality. Our fears about Cuba. The threat of a nuclear war. Our joyless life with the Tudors.

After acknowledging the deployment of nuclear weapons by the Soviets in Cuba, Kennedy ordered a quarantine of the island and encouraged other countries friendly to the United States to do the same. We knew this would have repercussions on the availability of consumer goods in Cuba, which was already inadequate since the economic embargo the U. S. had imposed on Cuba in 1961. As the two superpowers continued their negotiations, our worries about our families grew. All I could do was pray—I was becoming good at it.

Maybe my prayers were heard, for on October 28, President Kennedy reached an agreement with the Soviets. The missiles in Cuba would be dismantled and the United States would not invade Cuba or Russia.

A puzzling question remained: what will our parents do? After the agreement with Russia was reached, flights from Cuba to Miami were cancelled and all exit permits and waiver visas rendered invalid. In my mind, pictures of my parents' and sisters' passports and visas appeared shredded, confetti-like, for a carnival that would never be.

What could we do? No one would answer. Interest in reuniting *Pedro Pan* children with their parents had waned from public interest. The focus had turned to the failed Bay of Pigs attack. We heard rumors about negotiations between the U.S. government and Castro for the release of those captured in the attack in exchange for hard currency and goods that Fidel so desperately needed. Details about those negotiations were not made public and it took months before an agreement was reached. As we waited for an announcement, we cried for our parents and ourselves.

It was at this time that nightmares involving *papá* started to haunt me. They were always the same. After two, three, four or more days of his not coming back from the police station, I'd see him behind an explosion of white dust. The dust would settle on the ground, and I had to excavate to get him. What I would retrieve would be the broken head of a marble statue. Putting the pieces back together, I'd realize it was not *papá's* face I held in my hands. "Where's *papá*, where's *papá?*" I'd scream only to awake to a river of sweat covering my shaking body.

Time went by and Christmas came along, bringing with it a feeling of nostalgia for past holiday seasons. I remembered as a boy of eight or nine sitting on the floor of our home in Antilla a few days before Christmas, watching a miniature train set, a gift from my godmother for *El Día de los Reyes* (Three Kings Day). The train had stopped at a railroad crossing, and when the light turned green and the train moved on, my eyes followed its journey. Before it reached the station, the train veered off the tracks, ending on its side, wheels turning, motor moaning, whistle fading until it became but a whisper. "Walterio is on that train," I remembered saying. "I have to save him."

From the moment it entered our home, the train played a special role in our family's celebration of Christmas, becoming a much talked-about feature of the *nacimiento*, a project in which the whole family, with the exception of *papá*, would get involved.

Using the same cardboard boxes in which she had stored the figures for the *nacimiento*, *mamá* would shape the mountains and cover them in heavy paper she had dyed to a brownish color to resemble soil. The process would follow a familiar pattern year after year. After the mountains appeared, Beni, my sisters and I would take turns placing the houses, figures of shepherds, townspeople, Three Kings and their camels, and other animals throughout the village. Deciding what to place where often generated an argument. "No, move that house over here...it looks better there." Positioning the figures in the stable was another matter. *Mamá* took responsibility for that. The placement would never vary: Baby Jesus in the center; on his left, the Virgin Mary, and standing right behind her, Joseph. A small angel dressed in a flowing blue robe, an heirloom that had been in *mamá's* family since she was a young girl, would keep vigil from top of the stable. Placement of the train tracks would come next. When this was finished, we would place ornaments on a tree that stood next to the stable. It was time then to turn the train on—a job Beni and I would always fight over. Once we were done, we would watch the train chug along and whistle its way around the village, announcing Christmas had entered our home.

While at home we represented the nativity with a *nacimiento*, the Tudors, despite their religious fervor, brought Christmas into their home only with a six-foot tree they turned into a blinking distraction. Jesus, Mary, and Joseph appeared only in cards sent by relatives or friends that the Tudors piled at the bottom of the tree, or taped to the back of the front door.

What they made their own from the story of the birth of Jesus was the "no room at the inn" part. Certainly there was no room at the Tudors' for Beni and me.

In this country, part of the Christmas tradition entails the exchange of gifts, a practice not common in Cuba. There, Christmas was a religious holiday (though this stopped with Fidel.), celebrated with a midnight mass on December 24, and gifts, mostly for children, were distributed on the feast of the Epiphany, January 6, "Three Kings Day."

Although Beni and I were unaccustomed to the American tradition of gift-giving, the spirit of Christmas had infiltrated our senses since the day after Thanksgiving: carols attacking our ears around the clock; stores engaging our eyes with early Christmas displays; gift catalogues enticing our wallets.

Then, out of nowhere, a window burst open, and the scent and magic of Christmas vanished. The Tudors called a family meeting. We gathered around the dining table to hear the news: Mom Tudor's sister, Julie, whom we had never met, announced her husband had left her. Although she was not talking divorce—Catholics didn't like to—Julie expressed concern about how she would manage financially. Mom and Dad Tudor decided all the money they had planned to spend on Christmas would be sent to Julie instead. "This is a time to give. Julie needs us now. We are a family and we want to make this decision as a family. We want you guys to agree to this." The brothers hesitated at first but then nodded. Beni looked at me. I looked around and finally muttered a feeble "sure." Then we heard the brothers would fly to St. Paul the day after Christmas to spend time with their aunt. When Jon protested, Mom Tudor shot him a look that would have killed a Magi's camel.

Not only had our American Christmas vanished, but our Christmases in Cuba had become a memory I was afraid would fade away with time like fabric exposed to the sun. Many of our Cuban customs had already lost their vibrancy.

In Cuba, on New Year's Eve, as the clock chimed twelve midnight, we would eat *doces uvas* (twelve grapes), a grape with each stroke. The tradition had started in Spain and later spread to Cuba and other Latin American countries.

Finishing all twelve grapes by the last stroke meant a year of prosperity. Seldom, children could eat them all—it was a difficult task even for adults.

When I told the Tudors about the custom, they gave me a lecture on superstition, and I wondered if this family had turned its back on joy. "As a Catholic, there should be no room in your heart for those things. God takes care of your year, good or bad. It's what *He* chooses for you." I never told them about *mamá's* fascination, despite her Catholic upbringing, for attending séances, or having her future read by a fortune-teller.

I made it clear that superstition or not, twelve grapes would mark my midnight, and with money from my weekly allowance, I bought them—now twelve grapes, a dozen on each plate, waited for Beni and me in the refrigerator.

We won this tradition. Yet somehow having to fight for it had diminished my enthusiasm for keeping it alive.

This worried me. Our Cuban identity was having a slow death. As part of our *assimilation,* the Tudors had insisted on calling me Larry; now even classmates used the nickname to address me. Beni had become Ben. At first I had a hard time answering to Larry. I didn't know that person. In fact, because of the mask I wore to disguise my true self, particularly when it came to my sexual feelings, I hardly knew who I was.

It was two hours before midnight. Sprawled on the bed, I perused an old issue of *Life* magazine that I had read many times before. The pages stuck together. On the cover, the picture of Marilyn Monroe, who had died of an overdose the previous summer, showed greasy fingerprints and lines from unintended folding; inside, the articles spoke words I'd almost memorized.

On the window behind me, snow tapped a wistful wintry song. The weather had registered temperatures so low even the North Pole would complain, let alone two Cuban boys accustomed to weather never below the feel of warm tea. On nights like this I longed for my warm bed at home—even my bunk bed in Matecumbe. But, no, the Tudors' home claimed us.

I could hear Beni on the phone in the kitchen, his laughter fragile like a Christmas ornament that would break at the lightest touch. We hadn't said much to each other all evening, perhaps afraid our words would reveal a tree with no decorations, showing nothing but branches of pain. We wanted nothing like that. Not tonight.

The brothers had left for St. Paul, Minnesota, the day after Christmas to visit cousins they didn't like and celebrate with them holidays they would rather spend at home; Mom and Dad Tudor were out at the Johnsons'—one of the few friends they enjoyed spending time with, probably because they shared a disdain for alcohol. Why become numb to the pains of life, when life itself provided the only anesthesia they needed?

Right after the brothers left town, Mom and Dad Tudor—I had resigned myself to calling them that—announced their New Year's Eve plans excluded Beni and me. "The Tudor family has been invited to spend it with the Johnsons." We heard the line several times over several days. Beni and I would have to greet the New Year alone on South Benton Street, just the two of us, clicking our make-believe champagne glasses together and offering lonely walls in an uncaring house of a sleepy town a toast to the New Year. We were not allowed to drink—too young. We couldn't invite anyone over, either, or go out on our own. Strict orders!

I found it ironic we had participated in the decision about Julie "as a family," yet for the Johnsons' invitation, "family" meant only the Tudors.

The air in the room hung thick and cold, and the magazine provided only so much warmth. I put it down. Letters from Cuba I kept in a shoe box under my bed would provide some comfort. Their arrival had been sporadic since the Cuban missile crisis. I could reread them, as I'd done in the past when thoughts of not seeing my parents and sisters again would lodge in my stomach like a knife. But tonight, no, tonight I wanted to forget those letters. I'd keep them trapped inside the box; give them no air to breath. Yet the more I willed them away, the more they unfolded in front of my eyes, begging, *Read me, read me.* No!

In one of those letters, my twin had mentioned that since we left, neighbors shunned them, afraid to associate with them. That hurt. My mother had written of her happiness that our Christmas would unfold surrounded by such a "wonderful and generous family." That hurt even more.

Refusing to re-read those letters, and bored by the magazine, I decided to get up and check on Beni. His giggles had gained strength. He switched from Spanish to English and back in sentences that gave me no clue as to the person he was speaking to. I assumed it was Negrín, a *Pedro Pan* who lived in Richland with whom Beni often had long phone conversations. As I listened to Beni's bilingual fireworks, I realized how much our English had improved in just two months. On my first day of school, a classmate had escorted me to each of my classes, introducing me to teachers and students. I did not understand a word anyone said and could reply to questions only with a smile and a nod. Are you a communist? Nod. Are you from the moon? Nod. Are you stupid? Nod.

Not that anyone asked that, but who knew what I had said O.K. to? Regardless, I felt genuine warmth coming from teachers and students alike.

In Cuba, I had finished a fourth year of high school—high school was five years. I didn't continue because Fidel had closed all schools, so instead, I had concentrated on my music at the *conservatorio*. Here, the Tudors had decided to enroll me as a senior at Kennewick High. I needed to learn English (true) and take certain credits that were requirements to enter college in the state of Washington, such as American Government and Washington History (not sure it was true). They had enrolled Beni as a sophomore.

From the beginning, Beni and I scored well on school tests (better than Mike, so the Tudors asked we not gloat in front of him). I attributed our success to two factors: one, these were written tests (oral fluency, particularly for me, maybe because I was two years older, perhaps, took longer to achieve); two, Oteiza's lessons at Matecumbe had registered in our subconscious more than we realized.

Wearing the same dark corduroy pants he wore to dinner, Beni gave no indication of getting off the phone. The door to the family room was ajar; I could see the multi-color lights on the Christmas tree blinking an annoying rhythm. I wanted to turn them off. Instead, I took myself back to bed.

What time was it? The clock on the dresser marked ten-thirty. Not only was the arrival of midnight taking forever but Christmas itself had lasted an eternity. What's happened to *Joy to the World?* My legs fidgeted a choreography of boredom. Without getting out bed, I reached under and pulled out the box of letters. I would read them, after all. At that moment, the sound of the doorbell startled me. I jumped out of bed, sending the box of letters to the floor. Who could it be? Were the Tudors home early? Had they forgotten their key?

"No room at the inn," Beni yelled from the kitchen and continued talking on the phone.

I ran to the door, pajamas and all. When I opened it, a gust of cold wind swiped my face.

Peggy Anne, a girl around seventeen stood at the door. She and I had a few classes together. "Do you need a ride, Larry?" she asked, lingering on my name and parting her lips as if she were pouring honey from them. A fur beret tilted on her head reminded me of Marilyn on the cover of *Life*.

I wanted to tell her about the restrictions, no friends, no going out. But, the sight of her pushed my concerns aside. In less than a month I would turn nineteen; which meant I'd be out of the program, probably out on the streets. The Tudors were at the Johnsons. I was alone and restless in the bedroom. What did I have to lose?

A senior in high school, Peggy Anne owed her popularity in large part to owning a car, given to her by her father, and her willingness to drive students around on errands or just for fun. Once she gave a group of us a ride to a football game in Pasco; after the game, she and I found ourselves alone in the car. Urged by temptation, and a fleeting opportunity, we explored each other's bodies, until others interrupted, claiming their ride. Thoughts of Jorge Luís or El Havanero had disappeared behind a curtain of passionate kisses and probing hands. I wasn't sure what had happened to me then, but the idea of continuing on this New Year's Eve a test we had left unfinished intrigued me.

I ran inside, put on snow boots, then a jacket over my pajamas, and rushed out the door. Beni never got off the phone. I didn't know if he'd heard me when I said, "See you later."

When I slammed the door behind me, I realized I had left the grapes in the refrigerator, but, with Peggy Anne waiting for me in the car, such traditions seemed irrelevant.

Unimportant also were thoughts about past Christmases, letters, Beni, and the Tudors.

As Peggy Anne backed out of the snow-drenched driveway, the moon, trembling from the cold, turned its face away from us, as if embarrassed by our presence. In most places, the arrival of the New Year is observed with fireworks. Peggy Anne and I wouldn't need any artificial display to sparkle our celebration.

Mom and Dad Tudor, Happy New Year.

Chapter Sixteen

WITH THE ease of someone accustomed to driving in snow, Peggy Anne maneuvered the car past streets where colonial houses gave us a holiday greeting. Most windows had their drapes drawn to stop outsiders from intruding on their New Year's celebrations.

On East Columbia Drive, she turned right; a few blocks later, in a dark, isolated spot she halted the vehicle next to a tree, almost hugging it with the left side of the back fender. In front, across the Columbia River, lights from Pasco sparkled like a giant *nacimiento*; the moving traffic over the Pasco-Kennewick bridge reminded me of our miniature train set in Antilla.

Without exchanging a word, we got out of the car, ignoring the rain that had replaced earlier snow. We went around and jumped in the back. After throwing our jackets over the front seat, and in positions only contortionists would find comfortable, we kissed. The excitement escalated. I pushed the back of her blouse up and began to unhook her bra. My fingers had practiced many Chopin etudes but none like this. As I stumbled through the exercise, a light intruded upon us, scanning our bodies, then our faces. I lifted a hand to protect my eyes. Peeking through my fingers, I saw a policeman standing by the car window with flashlight in hand.

"What are you guys doing?" he asked while continuing to wave the light in our faces.

"Nothing, nothing," I said.

I'd not thought much about the Tudors before, but at that moment the possibility of Peggy Anne and I in the local precinct having to call them to bail us out froze my spine.

After Peggy Anne produced her license and car registration, and we gave an awkward promise to go straight home, the policeman let us go.

As we drove away, we settled into silence, neither of us knowing what to say about the shadow of desire still lingering in the car.

Had we continued on East Columbia Drive, we would have reached the bridge, maybe gone on to Pasco and become one more figure in the live *nacimiento*. Instead Peggy Anne turned left. We went past the high school and ended up back on South Denton on our way to the Tudors. Images of Jorge Luís, El Havanero, and Dario blinked in my eyes.

I'd rationalized my feelings for these men (one a boy, really) by placing them within the confines of desire rather than action. Were those feelings over forever? My experience with Peggy Anne had unleashed a kind of sexual hunger I barely recognized.

As I entered the living room around one in the morning, Beni lunged at me, thrusting a finger in my face, his eyes bulging, his nostrils steaming like an angry bull.

"Where were you? Where were you?"

"With Peggy Anne. I went for a ride."

"You didn't tell me."

"You wouldn't get off the phone," I said.

"You went with that *puta* and left me alone? I'm going out myself."

"Beni, you're not going anywhere."

"Watch me."

He went to the hall closet and yanked his winter coat off the hanger. I tried to wrestle it away from him. In the process he slipped on some snow I'd tracked in, and fell into a wiggly bundle on the floor, his coat next to him. Blood sprouted from his nose. The bull was wounded.

"Stay there," I said. "I'll get some Kleenex."

When I returned I knelt by his side, wiped the blood off his face, then pinched his nose to stop further bleeding.

"Don't," he screamed. "That hurts."

"This is how you do it." I remembered *abuela* saying you never tilt your head back during a nosebleed.

He pushed my hand away and tilted his head back, anyway.

Although winter had given Beni a few nosebleeds already, I felt responsible for the one tonight. *I should have eaten those twelve grapes.*

After a while, the bleeding stopped, and his breathing slowed down. "I thought you knew I was leaving. I should have made sure. Sorry."

"You always do what you want. You were always *mami's* favorite."

What? Mami's favorite? My decision to go with Peggy Anne was spontaneous, reckless in some ways. But, *mamá*, why, why was he bringing her into this? First he called Peggy Anne a *puta*, which I ignored, now it was all *mamá's* fault?

Growing up, Beni and I had endured a prickly sibling relationship. He'd accuse me of getting out of distributing flyers for *papá's* business, using the excuse I had to practice, and when *mamá* would keep me home because of some mischievous act I had committed, instead of hitting me, as Beni suggested, she would regale me with stories about her own *papá*. I remembered sitting cross-legged mesmerized by anecdotes about a man who played more than five instruments, an orchestra conductor, theatre director, a man who had left a legacy stamped on my forehead like a seal on an official document. What rang with a certain truth was the fact *I* was allowed to handle—or mishandle—*abuelo's* stamp collection. No one else was allowed to touch it.

But, did that make me *mamá's* favorite? Beni didn't know what I had done to *abuelo's* collection. In my mind, if someone was anybody's favorite, it was Beni. *Mamá* constantly reminded me, before we left Cuba and in her letters, to take care of him. And *papá*, well, he certainly had a soft spot for him. Both loved baseball and often talked about the game. Besides, *papá* saw Beni, rather than me, as his successor in the family business.

Crouching next to Beni, and hoping he'd get up soon so we could both go to bed, I had a view of the bottom half of a room so dull you'd fall asleep when you entered. Wooden legs from a low, long couch and a dark wood phonograph sank onto the wall-to-wall carpet like cargo from a shipwreck. While engulfed in that sea of blandness, I reassured Beni my action had nothing to do with my being anyone's favorite and repeated my apologies for leaving him alone. I vowed in the future to consider his needs before submitting to my own desires. Why allow anything, or anyone, even a girl like Peggy Anne, to fracture a responsibility I had accepted when Beni and I left Cuba.

I was at my most contrite when the front door creaked open. In seconds, two giant skyscrapers towered over us: Mom and Dad.

"What's all that blood?" Mom Tudor said, opening her eyes wide, and pointing to the bloody Kleenex in Beni's hand. By her reaction you would have thought she had entered a slaughterhouse.

"Were you boys fighting?" Dad Tudor said. Then, noticing I had my jacket on and Beni's rested on the floor by his side, he added, "Were you out? Didn't we say—"

"I slipped and got a bloody nose," Beni said.

"Clean this up, immediately," Mom Tudor said. She removed the dark gloves that matched her coat and the scarf that covered her head, making her look like a gypsy in a cheap Hollywood movie. "Then, go to bed, both of you. We will deal with this tomorrow. We can't leave you boys alone one night without you getting into trouble?" She looked at Dad Tudor, as if asking for support. He peered over his glasses and nodded.

In our bedroom, from a distance of at least five feet, Beni threw the Kleenex into the waste basket. It went in. A perfect shot.

Once in bed, thoughts of the Tudors crowded my mind. Why had Mom Tudor said "We can't leave you boys alone one night without you getting into trouble"? This implied previous transgressions, and nothing like tonight's episode had happened before. From the morning when Dad Tudor dropped us off to explore the empty house by ourselves, we had tried to accommodate to the foreign rituals of this family. To *assimilate*. And, we had received little recognition. I wondered how they would have reacted had I told them the truth about my experience with Peggy Anne. Well, I didn't care anymore. What was the worst thing that could happen? Beni and I would stand together against the Tudors.

"Good night, Beni, Happy New Year."

"Good night."

Chapter Seventeen

THE FOLLOWING morning, while we were still in bed, Beni's voice startled me: "Are you awake?" I pulled my blanket up, waved it in the air over my head a couple of times, and then submerged myself under it.

I could have been in Antilla playing the piano at the Union Club, attempting those Cuban rhythms that I didn't know but faked to the delight of most, or in Prague. If I were a tenor I would be singing *Nessum Dorma* from the opera *Turandot* (*Nobody shall sleep...Nobody shall sleep. Even you, o Princess, in your cold room*—I would dedicate it to Mom Tudor!).

But I felt far from a pianist these days, even after a performance of *Malagueña* at the high school talent show, which was well received, and for sure I was no tenor. Besides, after our experience the night before, I was in no mood to sing to Mom Tudor or anyone for that matter.

Accepting that further sleep was unlikely, I pulled the blanket off my face and turned toward Beni. "I'm kind of awake."

"I thought you had drowned under there." He gave an audible sigh. "Should we get up? I don't hear anyone..."

His words were interrupted by the flushing of the toilet from the bathroom adjacent to our bedroom.

I jerked myself up and beached against the wall behind me, my mind and body adopting a state of alert. "Let's get up. I'm really sorry about—"

He dismissed me with a friendly sweep of the hand. "My nose is still here, still big, still full, still crooked." A pause. "Are we in trouble?"

I nodded. I was not sure what to expect from the Tudors, but they seemed more unhinged than ever. Last night, after Beni and I put our coats back in the closet, they went to their room and delivered a perfunctory good night before closing the door behind them. The first time Dad Tudor didn't come to our room to pray with us.

No sense in delaying the inevitable, so after Beni and I gave each other a silent consent, he pushed his blanket off, stretched his legs way, way down, made a shoulder yawn, and got up. I followed suit. Once upright, we took turns using the bathroom. One person at a time was already a crowd in that room. Afterwards, we changed into slacks and sweaters we had bought from J.C. Penney with our own money.

When we got to the dining room, we found Dad Tudor seated at the table working on a bowl of cereal. In the narrow kitchen, which opened to the dining room, Mom Tudor busied herself, opening and closing the refrigerator without any apparent reason. Was she taking something out to eat or to cook? Something other than food seemed to preoccupy her.

Our good mornings were met by an icy stare and a nod from each of them.

We had been relegated to solitary confinement. What next? Water torture? Or better yet, execution? In England, in the sixteenth century, Henry VIII, the Tudor king, had ordered two of his six wives to be executed. I had loved this period of history when I studied it in Cuba, never knowing one day I might live it myself.

A week after New Year, we returned to school—the brothers were back already. When Beni and I got home that day, Dad Tudor sat us down at the dining table, which was already set for dinner. *Here it comes. The atomic bomb.* After some empty patter around the state of foreign politics and the importance of faith in our lives, he announced we would have a meeting the following day with Sra. González, a social worker, new to the job of helping *Pedro Pan* children in the area. We agreed with a bare nod of our heads and asked no questions. "She'll be here around the time you boys get home from school."

That night, anticipating the worst, I could hardly eat. Each mouthful, few as they were, was treated to a stare from one of the Tudors. It felt as though I were being watched by someone from the *Comité de Defensa de la Revolución,* hoping to catch me in some subversive activity. Mom Tudor's red blouse, missing the black in Fidel's flag, added discomfort to the scene. Each minute felt like an eternity, reminding me of our anxious time at immigration while we waited to learn about our future in this country—a fate that would bring us to the Tudors and eventually this unnerving moment. Despite my anxiety, the picture I presented was one of quiet submission, speaking only when spoken to; on the inside, however, I felt a revolution raging on.

Next afternoon, we assembled in the living room, all five of us, Mom and Dad Tudor, the social worker, Beni and I. Dad Tudor made the awkward introductions. "Ben, Larry, this is Sra. González...Sra. González, Beni and Larry...she's here to talk to you boys...boys, Sra. González wants to talk to you."

Sra. González tried to lighten the moment. *"Muchachos, parece que los alimentan bien.* It looks like they feed you well here." We knew she wasn't interested in discussing how well we were fed, and I wanted her to get on with it. She didn't disappoint. Beni and I had barely claimed our seats when she said, "Tell me about life with the Tudors."

"It's O.K.," Beni said, never taking his eyes off the floor. *Where have you been these past few months?*

"It's not easy," I said in Spanish.

"How can you say that?" Mom Tudor challenged me, curling her back like an alley cat ready to pounce. She must have understood the words, or perhaps the manner in which I delivered them. The tension in the room had more layers than a winter coat.

"Choor, choor," Sra. González said, her way of pronouncing the word *sure*. "But let them speak. You'll have plenty of opportunity to give me your side of the story." Mom Tudor narrowed her eyes. Sra. González left out that the Tudors had already given their side of the story, on the phone when they set up this meeting, and earlier before we arrived home.

"We don't seem to do anything right in their eyes, we're too loud, we disobey them, we're out of control, we're this, we're that. Even when it comes to school...we get better grades than Mike and Jon, and we can't mention it because it's not good for them.... they finally rented a piano, but I can't use it because they want to watch TV instead. The TV is next to the piano. I wanted to take art classes by correspondence, but they refused. It would cost money. What do they want?" By the time I was through, I was gasping for breath.

Mom Tudor took my silence as an opportunity to speak. "They've made no effort to integrate themselves into our family. They speak Spanish to each other so we don't understand what they say." What did she expect? Spanish was the language Beni and I felt the most comfortable in when we spoke to each other. We meant no disrespect.

With disappointment shading her words, Mom Tudor continued, "We have to ask them to clean their room. When they take baths they leave the bathroom a mess. One or the other is constantly on the phone. They are just not interested in making a future for themselves here…"

The litany went on, and although the words came from Mom, Dad Tudor bobbed his head in agreement.

Sra. González wrote something down on a yellow-lined pad.

Mom Tudor then mentioned her migraines. They were occurring so frequently she needed "to do something about it before it was too late." *Too late for what?* I never knew she suffered from migraines. I said nothing. I figured silence was my best ally at that point.

After she gave her signature "choor, choor" a few more times, Sra. González told us she would place us with another family. "What about my birthday? It's in three weeks. Will the new family take me in? Or will I be taken off the program? If so, what will happen to Beni? We can't be separated." I tried to keep my voice level.

"Let me handle all that," she said in tones that didn't reassure.

"We didn't do this for money," Dad Tudor said.

"Why did they do it?" I asked myself, silently.

Perhaps, the Tudors believed we would stay with them for only a short time (we all believed that), but after the Cuban missile crisis, when a reunion with our parents seemed unlikely, keeping us became an unanticipated burden. As I understood it, *Pedro Pans* were dismissed from the program the day they reached their nineteenth birthday. After that, the institution or family that cared for them no longer received financial support. Had this reality—I was about to turn nineteen— influenced the Tudors' decision?

How could I trust another experience with another American family? I wanted my own family here. But, Cubans could only come to the U.S. now through a third country, Mexico and Spain being the most popular. I asked Sra. González if she could help.

"Nothing I can do," she said. "You have to get visas to enter those countries in the country…and it's from spouse to spouse, children to parents or parents to children. It's complicated and expensive. How are you going to get there?" she asked, her tone dismissive.

I already knew that. I had written to *Padre* Palá about it and had received the same answer. Although I had accepted his response, Sra. González's reply, verging on the sarcastic, appalled me. My heart raced. My ears pounded. My vision blurred. I blurted out, "*Operación Pedro Pan* brought thousands of children out of Cuba. Shouldn't it bring our parents over now?"

She gave me a reprimanding stare. Then, she said in Spanish, "This is it." If we didn't fit in with our next family, she explained, we would be in big trouble and end up in a reform school or orphanage. The threat came as no surprise. Bouncing from family to family or ending up in an orphanage had happened to many *Pedro Pan* children. Even living with a relative had not proven to be stable. After a while, not able to care for the child any more, the relative would turn the child over to another family member, or back to the Catholic Welfare Bureau. In the case of siblings, the shuffling often resulted in the siblings being separated.

Although by El Havanero's experience, our placement did not qualify as a bad *beca,* I was hard put to classify it as a good one.

At least Beni and I were together, not in an orphanage, and not living with Carmen María and her predator husband. At the Tudors', our problems had emerged from the collision of two different cultures, rather than physical or sexual abuse.

After Sra. González left, I excused myself from dinner, went to the bedroom, and lay down. A letter from El Havanero sat on my bed. It had arrived earlier that day, but I couldn't bring myself to read it. I didn't want to hear about the orphanage. Our own experiences had upset me enough.

Beni ate with the Tudors, then joined the brothers in the den to watch the Red Skelton Show, a staple of American television at the time. In his mind all was forgotten or forgiven?

Later—I didn't know how much time had elapsed—I decided to get up to change into my pajamas. Beni was still out of the room. I went to the window, parted the curtains, and looked out. The tiny moon, attempting to brighten a sky that mirrored my despair, brought to mind the first movement of Beethoven's *Moonlight Sonata*—its melody dark and mysterious. It was the sound of a broken heart, after all Beethoven had written the composition for a pupil he had fallen in love with, who left him for someone else. And my heart was broken, not by the disillusionment of a failed romance, but by the disastrous end to our relationship with the Tudors. Were all American families like this? Cold? Indifferent? I knew the Petersons were not, but they had a Spanish lineage on Mrs. Peterson's mother's side that perhaps accounted for their warmth.

Beni's footsteps interrupted my musical reverie. "Hi," he said.

"How was dinner?" I asked without turning to him, my voice echoing the contour of Beethoven's haunting melody. I let go of the curtain and watched it drop on the window pane.

"O.K.," he said. Then ever the joker, he added, "I thought it was best to dump the arsenic you had reserved for the Tudors. Down the drain, I mean. And by the way, the grapes are still in the refrigerator. Shouldn't we eat them?" I realized they had been there since New Year's Eve. I gave him a faint smile and threw my mind back to the moon. A line floated through my head: *Moon, show me a place where love still reigns.*

I thought of writing the words down, but realized that in the morning I would end up discarding the piece of paper that had served as their cradle for the night, and Beni would retrieve it and make fun of me.

The holidays had disappointed. It was relieved only by the sight of Jacqueline Kennedy addressing the Bay of Pigs prisoners when Fidel returned them to the United States. The two governments had reached an agreement: the United States would pay a ransom of $53 million in food and medical supplies, donated by companies all over the country, in exchange for the prisoners' release. The deal almost collapsed at the last minute when Fidel demanded an additional $2.9 million in cash as the prisoners were ready to leave. In a frantic day of fundraising led by the president's brother, Attorney General Robert F. Kennedy, the money was raised. A tribute was held on December 29 at the Orange Bowl in Miami, and the First Lady addressed these men in Spanish, praising their valor; a speech that did much to restore the faith in Kennedy among Cubans in exile, and even among Americans. I wondered how Mr. O'Malley had reacted to the event, and in particular, to Kennedy's promise to these men he would one day return the Cuban flag to a free Cuba.

Watching the event on television was the one time during the holidays that a smile escaped my lips. Even the

Tudors acknowledged Jackie's participation with beaming eyes. I hoped all that money Fidel had received from the United States would help Cuba, and ultimately my parents.

When Beni and I went to bed, my thoughts turned to the Bay of Pigs prisoners. I decided if these men, who had been Fidel's political prisoners, had made it back to the United States, I would do whatever was necessary to bring my parents over, with or without the support of *Operación Pedro Pan,* Sra. González, or the Tudors.

Chapter Eighteen

FOUR MONTHS after arriving in their home, exactly one day after my 19th birthday, we said goodbye to the Tudors. Our new family, a second-generation, Polish couple in their mid-fifties, had a married daughter, Bobbi, living a few blocks away. Mrs. Kaminski, friendly, stout-bodied, and casual in her style of dressing, reminded me of a farmer's wife; Mr. Kaminski, tall and dour, walked with a limp, the result of a car accident in which their son, eleven or so at the time, died. Even when the Kaminskis reassured us they were not expecting us to replace the son they had lost, I wondered. The sadness that hovered over their souls was palpable. And although their warmth seemed genuine, our apprehension at becoming vulnerable again clouded many of our interactions with them.

Our attempts at assimilating to life in America had fizzled with the Tudors. Except that during our final goodbyes, they showered us with unexpected enthusiasm. "You must come and visit," Dad Tudor said, offering one of his rare smiles.

"Any time, any time," Mom Tudor interjected. "We're going to miss you so."

What had gone wrong? Why this sudden surge of affection when in fact they had just kicked us out onto the streets of a dark tomorrow?

Before we moved in with the Kaminskis, the Petersons offered to take me in. Because I would not agree to separate from Beni, I refused. Mrs. Peterson had already introduced me to Linda Purcell, a pianist and organist, who would become my lifeline to music while I was still with the Tudors and afterwards. She too proposed I move in with her, but since her invitation did not extend to Beni either, I declined that as well.

Three weeks after we left the Tudors, they invited us over for dinner. Out of curiosity I accepted. Beni refused. His avoidance of anything that made him uncomfortable would become a life-long habit.

Dining with the Tudors as a guest and not another member of the household eased some of the rancor I had felt toward them. They seemed concerned about Beni's health—I had offered the excuse he was not feeling well—and troubled about our inability to reunite with our parents, sounding authentic for the first time.

During dinner, I concluded the Tudors had acted impulsively, with the best of intentions, when the church requested volunteers to serve as foster parents to a pair of Cuban brothers. Given their reserved nature, the arrival in their home of a tropical cyclone that lasted longer than expected would become too much for them. Understanding and forgiving, however, did not erase our awkward experience with them, and to this day, the thought of it makes me cringe. At the time, we were two young men displaced from home in need of support and most of all love. From the Tudors we received neither.

When objectivity visits my thoughts—on those rare moments more likely to happen now as I look back— I blame circumstances. The *Pedro Pan* program needed to secure placements for children they had accepted into the program, whose numbers kept increasing daily. It didn't have the mechanism with which to prepare families for dealing with the children; the children themselves received no preparation for adapting to a new family and new culture. We were thrown together into the same pot like black beans and white rice. Although everyone hoped the results would turn as appetizing as the dish itself, often the rice would get burnt or too mushy from the beans.

The Kaminski's house was small and modest. With drawings I had made in art class, I personalized our bedroom, which was separated from a laundry area by a multi-colored curtain. A small table separated the two beds. On the table, a brass lamp shed a dim glow, under which it was difficult to read. Although Mr. Kaminski smoked, the family forbade *us* to smoke—in our bedroom, which we did anyway, or elsewhere in the house, which we didn't. Although we were careful to flush all cigarette butts down the toilet, I wondered why they never mentioned the smell of cigarette in our breaths, our clothes or even our room.

The Kaminskis made it clear they would not rent a piano, and, somehow, the pronouncement barely left a mark. I was grateful for what they offered. Their desire to provide a safe, tension-free environment felt authentic. Besides, even when the Tudors rented a piano, television interfered with my practicing and I had to rely on the availability of a piano at the high school, a room at a music store in Kennewick, whose owner Linda had introduced me to, or visits to Mrs. Peterson, or Linda. Both had beautiful grand pianos I enjoyed practicing on.

While not a beautiful woman, my trusted mentor Linda had a beauty of intention that appealed. Her nose was narrow and pointed like Alicia Alonso's, her smile generous and warm, her eyes soft and kind.

She and I talked for the most part about music or religion. Sometimes about Cuba, but often I found this topic too painful and would have to stop. We disagreed on composers. She adored Liszt; I preferred Chopin, Mozart and Beethoven. Although she played the organ for the Methodist Church and considered herself a Methodist, yoga satisfied a spiritual thirst her own religion couldn't quench. I wrestled with feelings about the Catholic Church, and voiced my doubts with awkward hesitation and a vagueness meant to distract her from my personal truth. I regret not allowing myself to soak in her experience with yoga and eastern philosophies. But, then you can't tell a child what lessons he might be missing by not opening himself to them. Only time and experience unlock those doors.

While still with the Tudors, I had applied to the music department of three different colleges. The Tudors insisted I go to a two-year college in Pasco. They had not asked that we move out yet. Linda had other ideas. She favored my going to Washington State University (WSU) to study with Jerry Bailey, whom she had met at several music conferences. "He's a wonderful teacher. That's where you belong." Even though music was not pulsing through my veins with the same rhythmic energy it once did, I still dreamed of going to the magical city of New York to study as Raúl had. As the entrance auditions approached, Linda offered to help, and I would spend weekends at her home, practicing and studying with her.

The schools had the same audition requirements: either a Bach prelude and fugue from the *Well-Tempered Clavier*, a major work from the classical period, most suggested a

Beethoven sonata; or a romantic piece, which could be substituted by a contemporary composition. I chose Beethoven's Sonata, popularly known as the *Les Adieux* (The Farewell or The Goodbyes). Beethoven had dedicated it to Archduke Rudolf after the French attack on Vienna by Napoléon Bonaparte in 1809, when the Archduke, Beethoven's patron, was forced to leave the city. Because of my experience as a refugee, I easily identified with the emotions evoked by Beethoven's writing in the first two movements. The euphoria of the ebullient finale (the Archduke's return), however, would remain something I could only hope for and imagine.

In contrast to the Kaminskis' and the Tudors', Linda's split-level home was attractive and spacious. The front door opened to a sunken area, where next to a large electric organ, a grand piano sat in front of French doors that opened to a well-manicured garden. On the right, three steps led to a large L-shaped living room. Handrails divided that part of the house from the area below, still allowing for a clear view of the piano and organ. From the elevated area, Mrs. Purcell's guests—they always included the Petersons—listened to my playing and offered a few hand waves, applause, and the occasional *bravo!* The accolades meant to inspire but somehow managed to instill a perspiration of nostalgia in my fingers.

These musical evenings, initially set up while I was preparing for my auditions, continued afterwards. I wondered if I would have felt the same melancholy had I been playing in a stranger's house in Prague. Would I miss Raúl and Jorge Luís? Yes, but the knowledge that in a year I'd return to Cuba would soothe my longing. Here, in Washington my future seemed uncharted, and although Linda offered mentoring and friendship, she could not fill the vacuum that the absence of family had made more pronounced since the missile crisis.

On a spring morning that must have forgotten the calendar, for it offered a chill that spoke of winter, Linda and I drove to Pullman—I had already auditioned for Whitman College in Spokane and Central Washington College in Ellensburg. Located in the southeastern part of the state, Pullman was only six miles west of the Idaho border.

I was still drowsy from a sleepless night when we entered the music building, a two-story, red-brick structure, next to the Library and cattycorner to Bryan Hall (a building with an imposing-looking tower with a clock on each of its four sides). We passed a glass vitrine, inside which were flyers announcing student and faculty recitals, and headed toward the wide stairs that led to the second floor. This was no colonial building but something about the place felt as familiar as the *conservatorio* in Santiago; perhaps it was the music coming from some of the rooms. Suddenly, the figure of a boy flying down the stairs almost collided with us.

"Hi," the boy said with an exultant cry. The clean scent of someone who had just taken a shower tickled my nostrils. He took a step back and studied my face, then the rest of me. His gaze bore holes up and down my body. "It is you!" Of course it was me. Who else? But, who was he? Some sort of ghost. Except, his fetching eyes, as Linda later referred to them, were not features associated with a spook or ogre.

I introduced myself and then said, "Meet Mrs. Purcell."

"Please call me Linda."

"You're Larry," he said.

"How do you—"

"Jerry showed me your picture."

What was he talking about?

"Must have been the picture I sent with your application," Linda said.

I forced an amused expression. "I'm Chuck," he said. "I study with Jerry. Hope you get him…I know he's been looking forward to meeting you…he's great…I was looking for Annie, but then I saw…you!"

He thundered a wink that exploded inside me. "I don't know Annie. I don't know… anyone here," I said.

He brushed off a clump of blond hair from his forehead, then exited, saying, "I have to find Annie, we're playing Brahms' *Liebeslieder Waltzes*." The encounter had shaken me up —Linda couldn't figure out why, and neither could I. Actually, I could. Although the two boys were worlds apart in looks, I had reacted to Chuck in a similar way I had to El Havanero. El Havanero had a strong physique with a dark, mediterranean air. Chuck, on the other hand, was tall, lean and agile in a short-distance runner sort of way. His leather jacket over the blue jeans, meant to give him a James Dean aura, succeeded only in showing a kid from a Leave-it-to-Beaver neighborhood trying to look tough.

Aware of my uneasiness Linda said, "Think of nothing but the music, note by note, sound by sound. Inhale…exhale…" She cupped her hands over mine. Her words hypnotized me, and I took deep breaths. After a while, with Chuck exhaled out of my mind, I walked into the audition room, where three stern-looking men sat on a long couch with note pads on their laps. Facing the men were two Grand Steinways placed side by side. They introduced themselves, Dr. Bailey, Dr. Brandt, Dr. Stout. All wore glasses, all had dark suits on, all delivered tight grins. I had barely finished the first movement of the Beethoven Sonata, when Dr. Bailey said they'd heard enough. Was this a quick win, or a flat-out disaster?

A month and a half after the audition at WSU, I heard from all three schools. I was accepted by all of them. Two offered partial scholarships. Washington State University, on the other hand, provided enough financial aid to cover my full tuition. The news was refreshing, as if I had just showered the salt off my body after swimming in the ocean. But, I still had to pay for my room and board. The issue was solved after Linda spoke to Dr. Stout, then dean of the Music Department, and he agreed to let me live with his family rent-free in exchange for daily chores.

By this time, after the missile crisis, Cuba's complete isolation imposed by the U.S. was in effect and the internal situation in the island had become desperate. Shouldn't I move to Mexico or Spain instead of going to college? According to *Padre*, and *Sra.* González, this was the only way to get my parents here. Had I not promised *mamá* in the lobby of the Lincoln Hotel that I'd do whatever was necessary to help the family? What was I doing now going to college and forgetting about them?

"This is what your parents would want for you," Linda said. No matter how often she reassured me, my parents' plight continued to play a painful melody in my mind; separating from Beni also concerned me. Already, the link that joined us had begun to corrode.

Graduation time came, and the picture that appeared in the paper showed row after row of caps and gowns waiting to be called to the podium to receive their diplomas. I sent the clipping to Cuba with an X marking my spot. What the picture didn't show was that, despite the Tudors' claims we were doing nothing to improve our lot in this country—they didn't attend the ceremony—I ranked 10th in a class of close to three hundred students, receiving the highest grade in my English final. What an irony considering I was new to the language.

I spent the summer between graduation and my first semester in college as a counselor for a music camp held on the WSU campus. Chuck was a counselor as well, and my encounters with him continued to evoke feelings I still found disconcerting.

One Sunday, I performed for visiting parents, earning a review in the Yakima paper: *The best performance of the concert was Lorenzo Martinez's interpretation of Chopin's Fantasie Impromptu.*

Chuck brought the clipping over. I made a copy of the review and sent it to Cuba with a request my parents share it with Raúl. That night, I danced in the privacy of my room, thrusting a victory fist into the air until tears of happiness threw me in bed and I fell asleep. I'd turned a *beca* that was only inches away from disaster into triumph.

Back in the Tri-Cities, I noticed Beni's relationship with the Kaminskis was now curdling. The possibility of another Tudor-like experience for him worried me. A call from Cuba, received only days before I left for WSU to start my freshman year, added overtones to my qualms about leaving him behind and produced new worries about my parents.

"Fidel took *papá's* business," Tere said.

"*Muchacha,* why would you say something like that?" *mamá's* muffled voice said in the background.

"Well, it's true," Tere insisted.

"What happened? How did it—"

"We were walking to the train station...going to Santiago," Tere said. "I saw *milicianos* sitting outside the store. I didn't want to say anything then...but..."

"*Niña,* give me the phone," *mamá* said and took the phone away from Tere.

"*Mamá*, tell me. It's too late to pretend it didn't happen," I said, remembering *mamá's* prediction, as well as the jewelry they had put aside to sell so they could survive financially during this time.

"Your *papi es fuerte*, a strong man. But of course, to see what you've worked so hard all your life taken away like that hurts." Her voice then changed from disappointment to contentment in less than a beat. "We're doing well. Spending now most of our time in Santiago with your *abuela*. We got the picture of your graduation. So proud of you!"

I didn't want to press for more information. Someone was probably eavesdropping.

When the call ended, my heart felt hollow, as if it had been emptied to take in all the tears of the world. I thought of *papá*, how he had predicted the end of his future in Cuba as a business man, as a citizen, unable to express his personal and political views, and how I had for a long time ignored his predicament. Now I wept for him and many others like him, who might have lost businesses they had worked for all their lives. I wept also for the Cuban children who had lost their childhood to Fidel and whose tears, like mine, could not bring a reunion with family. Could we grow wings that would fly us back home so we could kiss once again the mother who gave us birth, the father who hid his fears behind a façade of strength and determination, the sisters who prayed every night for a miracle to bring us together again?

When the fall semester at WSU started, I wore my grief over my parents' situation in Cuba as if it were a winter coat protecting me from the cold. Only the occasional call to Linda, or Mrs. Peterson, removed a layer or two from the sad garment. The effect, however, was temporary. I lost weight, my posture sagged, my concentration suffered, practicing lost its appeal, asthma tightened around my chest.

During this time, I only heard from Beni if I initiated a phone call, and news from home became infrequent. Because letters came through a third country, they took longer to arrive; often they were censored, with most of the writing crossed out in black ink. Whatever mail I received, I sent to Beni, but since we were no longer together where he could just sign his name to my letters, my parents didn't hear from him.

Sometimes, the saddest moments in life serve to take us out of our own melancholy. That's exactly what happened on Friday, November 22, 1963, a year after our arrival in the Tri-Cities area.

I was in Geology class at WSU when someone walked in, somber and ashen-faced, interrupting the teacher. "President Kennedy has been shot," the chubby figure, with pants clumsily held in place by black suspenders, announced to a stunned class. Over the next few days, in a state of disbelief, I shared with the country and the rest of the world, the profound grief this tragic event inflicted upon all, young and old, students and teachers, Democrats and Republicans. I imagined that even in Cuba, many were mourning the loss of this President whose charisma among political leaders perhaps only Fidel could match. Even in our house, where President Kennedy was not loved, mostly on *papá's* part, he, as well as *mamá*, would have condemned the heinous act that ended the life of a president, a husband and a father. After all, the man who had betrayed the Cubans at Bay of Pigs had averted a nuclear war when he confronted the Soviet Union over the construction of missile bases in Cuba. In many ways, we owed him our lives. *Papá* and *mamá*,

I expected, would put aside their grudges. It became clear the Russians didn't hold any resentment toward the man who had called their bluff during the Cuban Missile crisis; they sent First Deputy Premier Anastas Mikoyan to represent their country at the President's funeral. Cuba, of course, was absent from the solemn ceremony because of Castro's deep-seated hatred toward Kennedy and anything American—despite Kennedy's support of the Cuban economy when he provided millions in food and medicine, and even cash, in exchange for the return of the Bay of Pigs prisoners.

Hearing the Air Force Band play a transcription of Chopin's *Funeral March* made me weep like a child, my grief compounded when I saw the image of a little boy saluting his father's casket.

The picture of that boy saying goodbye to his past made me reassess my own life. How could I be unhappy about my lot in the U.S. when a boy, his sister, his mother faced their destiny with such dignity—a future that not only affected them but the life of this country and the world as well. They had each other, as I had Beni, even if he had turned the relatively short distance between Kennewick and Pullman into a gulf of silence. Besides, my family was still alive. If Mrs. Kennedy and her children could resign themselves to their pain with such grace, why couldn't I? Could I stop viewing the path my life had taken as a torturous road and see it instead as a conduit to a future of freedom and happiness?

That night, I went to visit Chuck in his dorm room. Grief cried on our faces. We hugged, comforting each other's shaking shoulders. Then, in a move that was both surprising and spontaneous, we kissed; at that moment, all pain disappeared.

On our fourth birthday. *Mamá* is behind Tere. Beni is in front.

Tere's ninth birthday.

On our front porch on our way to a costume party.

Los rumberos. I'm second from right on second row.

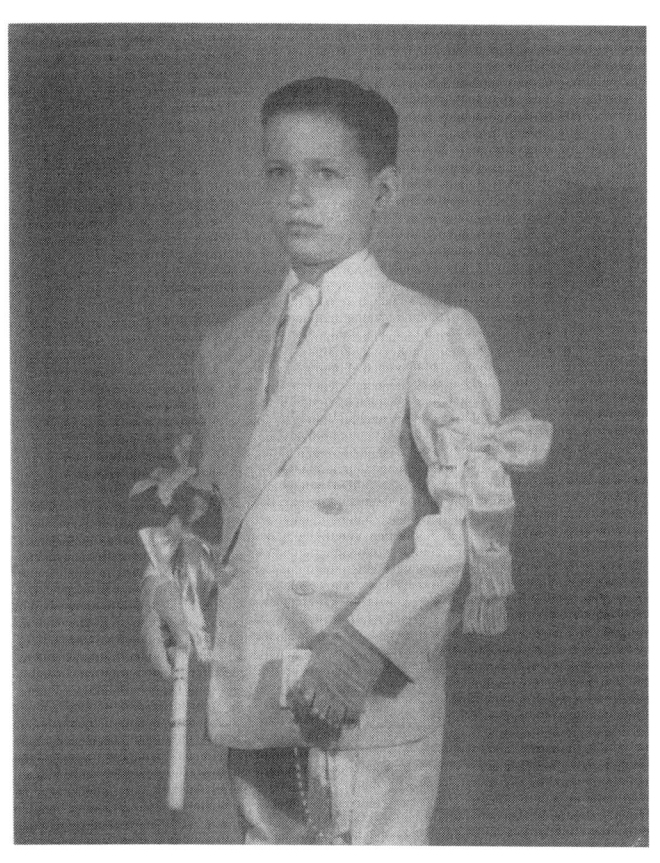

My first communion (9 years old).

Beni (kneeling third from right) with his baseball team in Antilla.

Betty and I doing a Cuban *zapateo* for a school performance.

As first lady of the Rotary Club (*papá* was
president), *mamá* organized a food drive.
Here she's delivering groceries to one of the beneficiaries.

Papá, second from left, placing flowers on the statue of Martí.

In front of our tent at Matecumbe. I'm kneeling, second from right. Behind me is Darío.

Standing in the Tudors' backyard.

Third Movement
The Reunion

Chapter Nineteen

THE YEAR before we met, Chuck joined the Mormon Church. At first, he didn't take his commitment seriously, but a renewed interest in the Church's doctrines, which he expected me to embrace as my own, had cooled off the physical side of our relationship.

"I can't do this," I said as I studied the oversized wood table where the four of us sat: the two missionaries, Chuck, and I. Maybe it was the table's size or the smallness of the room, or both that made me feel as if the paneled walls were caving in.

"You're not going to sign?" Chuck asked.

From the beginning I doubted I'd go through with this, despite my promises to go into the lessons with an "open mind." Now I had to tell them, and I was afraid my decision would end my relationship with Chuck, which was already limping along, and my bond with these two missionaries, who at the beginning made me feel as if they were friends, compassionate, concerned about my story, willing to fill in the gap of family. I realized that to them I was nothing but a fish they wanted to reel in, much like the marlin in Hemingway's *The Old Man and the Sea*. Although I probably led them to believe they would find an easy catch, unlike the fish in Hemingway's story, I would avoid an encounter with the harpoon.

"I can't get baptized," I said, my hands going up in a sign of frustration.

"Have you prayed?" Chuck, who was seated to my left, asked. I threw him a glance. All color had drained from his face. The missionaries' faces, on the other hand, remained impassive.

"I've done enough of that. Praying, I mean."

The taller of the two missionaries wrestled the Book of Mormon from the table, the cover toward me. "To be considered a member in good standing, the Church expects—"

"I know what the Church expects. It's all nonsense," I said. After an awkward silence, I continued, "O.K., so now I sign...I agree to be baptized, what next? Become a missionary?" The missionary holding the Book of Mormon closed his eyes and twisted his mouth, reminding me of a child who had opened a package to find a present not to his liking. "Two years out of my life? Send me to Mexico or Spain on a mission and then we'll talk, but otherwise...I came here as a refugee in search of freedom for me, my brother, and ultimately my family...not to take two years out of my life to evangelize, to indoctrinate others. I might as well recruit you, all of you, to fight communism. Let's go, let's overthrow Fidel's regime and bring my family over. What do you think of that?"

After my tirade, I got up, making it clear the concert was over. As my steps took me out of the building, leaving a perplexed trio behind, victorious echoes of Beethoven's *Ode to Joy* played in my mind.

Had I known the fate Chuck would eventually meet—he was one of the early casualties of the AIDS epidemic—perhaps I might have reacted in a less aggressive manner. But I was as blind to a pandemic that in a couple of decades would devastate the gay community as the whole world was. That

I was willing to replace the doctrines of my own religion, which I found narrow-minded, for another just as intolerant was the result of a boy desperate to belong, to be accepted, to be loved.

The building right behind the music department, where students used to practice, had been demolished to give way to a new structure that would hold classrooms, practice rooms, offices and its own auditorium. While waiting for its completion, we used an old house, down the hill behind the library that was better suited for scrap wood than practice rooms.

The walls were paper-thin. When you entered the long, narrow corridor, music tumbled out of each room. One sound on top of the other—the musical equivalent to a human pyramid. Once you peeled each tier off you recognized the work and who was practicing. That afternoon, the first room on the left offered the broken triad of Mozart's Sonata in F. That was Annie. From the adjacent room came the rich texture of a Brahms' Rhapsody. That was Glenn, a boy from the Midwest who was majoring in agriculture but took lessons from Jerry. On the right, from a room halfway down the hall, the familiar opening of Rachmaninoff's Second Piano Concerto pealed through the door. The bell-like chords then resolved into arpeggios over which the orchestra would play the first theme. That was Chuck. It had been three weeks since my meeting with him and the missionaries, and the frigid indifference that had extended between us had begun to thaw.

As I opened the door, Chuck turned his head toward me, but continued playing.

I took this as my cue to retreat.

"No, no. Stay," he said, his fingers still articulating the music of the concerto.

What gives?

Seconds later, he stopped in mid-passage.

"Sounds great," I said.

"Not so clean. The fingering." His eyebrows lifted, then he added, "I told Jerry."

I didn't know what he was talking about. Did he tell Jerry he was having problems with this passage? The part he had just abandoned was like filigree to warm the pianist's fingers. Over the piano part, the orchestra would play the theme. That's what people heard. The orchestra. The beautiful melody. It didn't matter what the pianist played there. He could have played *Three Blind Mice* and no one would have noticed. How unfortunate that he had so little confidence in his playing. He was a much better pianist than I was.

His next words clarified it all. "I'm going on a mission. The Church is going to help pay for it. I'm still working on my family."

I wanted to tell him he was making a mistake. That he belonged here. In music. But I realized my words would have no impact. He was going to leave no matter what. I had looked up to him, believed in him. Loved him? Probably not. But at the time, I thought I did. And the feeling was so strong, I had done the unthinkable. Lied to him. About my intentions to become a member of a Church I knew deep inside I would never join.

Another *adiós*.

I realized I had to go on, though. I'd had plenty of practice shedding relationships. That was what all *Pedro Pans* learned to do. I'd already shed several: my parents'; Jorge Luis'; El Havanero's; friends' from camp; even Beni's.

What neither Chuck nor I realized was that by his introducing me a couple of months earlier to a Pullman family, he had opened doors to a friendship that would assuage my melancholy during his absence and define my future in this town.

It was a shivering winter evening during the Christmas break of my freshman year. The campus had emptied out. Chuck was a rare ornament left at his dorm among a handful of others who had no family to go to, or from whom they wanted to escape.

Because of Chuck's disdain for his own, Bonnie and Remo Fausti became his surrogate family. Attractive, well-dressed, her hair and lips a bright red, Bonnie was a Lucille Ball lookalike. She worked part-time in the Library of Veterinary, spoke a bit of Spanish and French, loved music (had taken piano lessons as a child), and was solicitous and protective of Chuck. But then again, Bonnie was known to open her home and heart to any talented student in need of a shoulder to cry on, or a good meal. Lucky for me! But, there was a catch. You had to play for your meal. In my case, a barbeque of hamburgers and baked beans meant Chopin's *Barcarolle;* a full dinner featuring one of her Italian specialties a full Beethoven sonata.

The moment we entered their home, the Faustis' holiday excitement wrapped around me like ribbon on a present. Daughter Jan was busy in the kitchen, making peanut brittle, a family recipe she prepared every Christmas; Chuck had gone to the den to speak to Bonnie's husband. Without much of a preamble, I helped Jan measure ingredients: water, sugar, syrup, peanuts, everything. "Bringing the brittle to the right temperature is key," Jan said. When the concoction registered 300 degree Fahrenheit on the candy thermometer, we added the butter and vanilla; then we spread it out on a buttered baking sheet to let it cool. This was such a different Christmas from the one the year before.

The Faustis lived in a residential part of town, up the hill—a treacherous drive down on a snowy day—only three or four houses away from the Stouts, where I shared a simple but comfortable room with another student, Mike. The Stouts were building a new home across town to which we would move as soon as it was finished. I liked the old home, though, because of its proximity to the Faustis. In the dark, late at night, when most of the neighborhood slept, I could have walked over in my pajamas and no one would have noticed. When the Stouts' new house, closer to campus, was ready, the move fenced me in. Bonnie, however, drove me to and from her house in her small red Volkswagen.

I could speak to Bonnie about almost anything: Chuck—I believed she knew what was going on between us (she never mentioned it, though, and I never explained); my curiosity about the Mormon Church; my family in Cuba; Beni. It was as if I would present her with a sink full of dishes, and she would help me soak those that needed soaking, dry those that were already washed, then help me put them away. When I mentioned my guilt about leaving Beni behind, she would say, "You can't live for others. You do what you can." She believed Beni's rebellion, lack of interest in family, and apathy toward school were typical teenage reactions. "One of these days, he'll make a total turnaround. It will surprise you." Her optimism did not parallel mine.

Because of his constant Richland escapades ("I'm not stopping."), the Kaminskis had threatened to have the social worker transfer Beni to a family in Mabton (a farming community in eastern Washington close to Yakima); according to them, no other family would take him. I pictured Beni in overalls picking cotton (is that what they pick in this part of the state? Or was it corn? Maybe celery?); the image of Beni picking something or other, or sitting on a tiny stool milking cows, seemed as a distorted as a Dali painting.

Beni decided to call the Kaminskis' bluff. His best friend in Richland, Negrín, lived with the McCauleys, who were parents in the *Pedro Pan* program and were willing to take Beni in. His decision was precipitated by his meeting Cindy Craig at a party in Richland. He wanted to be close to her. The McCauleys had a house-full already: eight kids of their own, besides Negrín, his sister Sylvia and now Beni. "Beni, this is not a home. It's a rabbit's nest. Are you sure you want to do this?"

My advice went nowhere. Beni moved in with the McCauleys. On Beni's behalf, I can say that despite his disagreements with the Kaminskis, he had great respect for them, and even after he moved out, continued to visit them, something he never did with the Tudors.

At the end of my freshman year, Chuck had already announced he was leaving on his mission, and Beni had not yet moved to Richland, the contour of my life was about to change. Again.

I was in my room getting dressed when the upstairs doorbell made me lift my head toward the sound. My room at the Stouts' new home was in the basement, which opened to the outside, but "the formal entrance," as Mrs. Stout called it, was on the first floor. To get to it you had to take the stairs that rose from street level and twisted twice in the air until it landed at the front door. Most people rang the basement bell, or just knocked, much easier that trekking all the way up, but today the visitor chose to climb those awkward steps.

"Larry, you have a telegram," Mrs. Stout called from upstairs.

It was not my birthday or a special holiday. This could only mean…what?

I remembered the day *abuela* presented me with the telegram, and as I took the one from Mrs. Stout, my body shivered as if from a fever. After a mere thank you, I went back to my room.

There are times when intuition tells you what you're about to learn will change your life in unimaginable ways. This was one of those moments.

I plunged the weight of my body down on the soft bed; then with one eye open, as if to absorb only half the news, I read the telegram aloud, a word at a time. *Tia. Chuchi. Betty. And. Tere. Arrive. In. Mexico. Tomorrow.*

I stayed quiet for a few seconds, tossing the words in my mind. The moment seemed to stretch from my room to the end of the world. I wondered how they had done it. One day, my aunt and sisters were trapped in Cuba, the next they were on their way to Mexico. What about my parents? Why not them as well?

Another question bore a hole in my head. How would I be able to help them? They would not qualify for *Operación Pedro Pan*. The program was for all practical purposes over. Only those who were already part of it continued receiving support, like Beni. I was on my own, living with the Stouts.

As I hiked over to campus, I felt as if I were sleepwalking, aware and not aware of myself or my surroundings. My head floated above me like balloon on a string, my legs marched me in military-like steps down Orchard Street, past the Mormon Church. I recalled staggering in the same stupor-like state from *abuela's* apartment looking for Raúl and Jorge Luís the day I received my exit telegram.

Before I knew it, I was trooping along the northeastern edge of Compton Union Building (CUB), a hub for student activities, where love was declared, relationships broken, meals eaten, books read, and large celebrations, particularly homecoming events, held. I could go in and get lost in the noisy air of the place, or keep on walking until I reached the back of the library and then make my way toward the music building. I could find someone there with whom I could talk. Maybe I should go home and call Beni. He wouldn't be home, but I'd tell the Kaminskis, and they would let him know. I should also tell Mrs. Stout. I had left without mentioning what the telegram said. At that moment, a group of students, three or four, in a single line, headed toward me, crowding the narrow winding corridor on this side of the CUB. My vision dimmed; the scene in front of me blurred. The students had transformed themselves into children playing a game I remembered well, a game that had made its way from France to Spain to Cuba and then to other Latin American countries:

A mambró cható materile-rile-rile
A mambró cható materile-rile-ron
Yo tengo un castillo, materile-rile-rile
Yo tengo un castillo, materile-rile-rón.

(I have a castle, materile-rile-rile
I have a castle, materile-rile-rón.)

In the game, several children formed a line and a single child faced them. After the *materile* refrain, the single child would sing the line, "I have a castle," and the group would ask where the keys to the castle were. *En el fondo del mar* (At the bottom of the sea), the child would reply and then select someone from the group to find the keys.

When the students passed me, their talk of an upcoming Chemistry exam brought me out of my playful reverie, reminding me of my own Music History test scheduled for the following day. But I couldn't worry about exams. Not now. Only of finding the keys to the castle. *At the bottom of the sea,* the refrain sang in my head. "But where, where is that god damn castle?" I yelled, flailing my arms like a mad man. I continued screaming, "And the key... I've got to find the key...the castle and the key...help me find them!" I ran off toward the music building.

Chapter Twenty

FIVE AND a half months after I received the telegram, Betty and Tere sat at the Stouts' dining table, which had made the move to the new house and perhaps shouldn't have. "It's an antique," Mrs. Stout said. I knew nothing about antiques. To me, it was an old, decrepit piece, probably rescued from Noah's Ark, that exhibited scratches and grooves Mrs. Stout disguised with colorful tablecloths she kept in a cabinet nearby.

Joining us for dinner were Bonnie, her daughter Jan, and Barrett, the Stouts' son, also a student at WSU. Although he knew Jan from the time both families lived up the hill close to each other, he had paid little attention to her in the past. She was the little girl you said hello to out of politeness, commenting on how cute and smart she was, and then ignored for the rest of the evening. Not tonight.

Barrett's eyes sparkled as he assessed the poised young lady seated to his right. The awkward flower girl had metamorphosed into a swan, Eliza in Shaw's *Pygmalion*. Despite his interest in Jan, which he couldn't hide even under a pile of stones, he was paying attention to my sisters; his curiosity in their stories rang with interested laughter. Perhaps he was trying to impress Jan by showing a caring young man rather than the aloof, brooding person most people thought of when describing him. He found Betty's ability to spin a story, even with her limited English, amusing, and encouraged her to go on; at times, he helped her find the right word in a Spanish-English dictionary she kept above her knife for easy reach.

    The Stouts were traveling and had allowed my sisters to use the master bedroom for a couple of days until we moved into the apartment Bonnie had helped me get ready for the three of us. In true *Materile* fashion, she had found both the castle and the key to unlock it. When I mentioned the telegram and the dilemma I was in, she offered to take me to Father Durand, the local Catholic priest, whom I had met several times at dinners at her home. "He might have some ideas."

    Father was a jovial-looking man, his eyes open and friendly, his dark hair a halo of curls around his round face. He liked his wines red, the color of his cheeks. His voice, accustomed to telling jokes, some a bit off-color, never rose above a whisper, probably the result of years at the confessionary trying to keep private exchanges between him and the person seeking absolution. When I went to him, I felt disingenuous. How could I ask help from someone who represented a faith whose values I had rejected? I had no choice. So, when Father offered, rent-free for year, an apartment the church owned, I accepted. His generosity was a gift from God; my acceptance more like an act of prostitution. *Forgive me, Father, for I have sinned.*

    Besides *tía* Chuchi, who stayed in Miami—she couldn't imagine spending a winter in the cold northwest—missing from dinner was Beni; he was in Richland attending classes and by then living with the McCauleys. We called him when my sisters arrived. On my sisters' side of the conversation, side-splitting laughter filled the air in reaction to jokes he delivered. *What's so funny?* With so much going on, I hadn't had time to ask about the call. What I cared to know was why he was not here. He had refused to accept the Tudors' invitation for dinner because it was an uncomfortable situation. Was our sisters' arrival another awkward moment he preferred to avoid? He had left everything to me, from finding the apartment to getting it ready to figuring out how we were going to afford it all. It was natural the responsibility would fall on my shoulders. I was older. On the other hand, he could have spent one of his weekends painting or moving furniture, but baseball games and Cindy kept him "too busy." When I would phone him to report on progress, he would offer monosyllabic responses: "Good."

Everyone at the table wanted to hear about my sisters' experience in Mexico. Although I was familiar with it—they had written about it in letters—their words, now delivered only a few feet away, created a renewed poignancy, like a book that feels fresh upon rereading. We couldn't turn the pages fast enough.

The visas they obtained to enter Mexico were fake, bought by *papá* in the black market. How much he paid for them, they weren't sure. Tere, my older sister, said, "In Cuba those things happen but you don't know exactly how. 'Here are visas. You go to Mexico.' You don't bother to ask. If you ask, you get '*un buen amigo.*' Everything happens through *un buen amigo.*"

I recalled my own *buenos amigos* who had made Beni's and my visa to this country possible: Sister Margarita, Alicia Alonso's sister—all part of the clandestine network working to get children out of Cuba. When this subversive movement collapsed, Cubans figured ways to enter the United States through a third country. Even if it meant fake visas.

Resorting to illegal means to flee the island would become commonplace. The most notorious case, perhaps to this day, is Elián González's. On Thanksgiving 2000, a fisherman found Elián, seven years old at the time, clinging to an inner tube off the Florida coast. His mother and others fleeing Cuba had drowned on that same perilous journey. Elián went to live with relatives in Miami; however, his father, who was separated from his mother and had remained in Cuba, claimed that Elián was taken against his consent and demanded that the boy be sent back. The U.S. legal system ruled in the father's favor, but Elián's Miami relatives refused to relinquish him. Five months after Elián's death-defying journey, federal agents raided the boy's uncle's house and took Elián at gunpoint. Shortly thereafter, he returned to Cuba.

In Mexico, my sisters lived on Calle Universidad with *la señorita*, a spinster in her fifties, educated, a Mexican citizen of European background. Staying with *la señorita* was a niece. "Pretty, blond like *la señorita*," Tere said. "They were French or something. Not Mexican."

It was a two-storied house, although they didn't know how many rooms it had because no one was allowed into the part of the house where *la señorita* and her niece lived. The women, five in all, slept in makeshift accommodations in the garage on army cots; between cots, sheets floated down from the ceiling pretending to afford them some privacy.

"Other Cubans stayed in house, too," Betty said. "Men. They slept upstairs. We no go there, either."

When Barrett asked what they did in Mexico every day, pain flushed over Betty's face. She mentioned they went to *Gobernación* every morning to ask for our parents' visas but always returned empty-handed. After two months, my sisters' permit to enter the United States arrived. Tere and *tía* Chuchi left for Miami. *El Refugio,* which paid for their stay at *la señorita's,* would not continue supporting all three. "Only one. Only one could stay to get visas for *mami* and *papi*. I stay. Three months more. Alone..." At the word alone, Betty's voice shattered like glass. "I almost gave up...no luck everyday *gobernación*. Then *papá* sent telegram." She sighed. "Lawyer, friend of *papá's* friend was going to help. But lawyer wanted me in hotel. With him. I called *papá*. Crying. He called his friend. His friend called lawyer. Following day, visas on their way to Cuba. Not good that man!" With her napkin she dabbed a tear from the corner of her eye.

I thought of El Havanero, the maltreatment he had received in the orphanage, and the abuses, sexual and otherwise, so many young Cubans had endured in the name of freedom—even Beni had experienced an unpleasant overture from *papá's* cousin's husband. As refugees, we often found ourselves in a dance where outside forces would step on our toes; after each misstep, we'd recover and get on with the dance—as far away as possible from the offending partner.

While I cleared the table, with Jan's and Barrett's help, Bonnie talked to my sisters. A bit of Spanish from her, a bit of English from them. Bonnie explained about the apartment, reminding them it was rent free for a year; we were responsible for everything else. "No more *sábanas*. No sheets between your beds. Completely furnished." My sisters nodded. I believed they understood, although I had already explained it all to them. "You will get jobs, and Larry is already making some money."

She was right. I was paid for accompanying students' recitals and playing the chimes at Bryan Hall, a job I inherited from Chuck, which I did every night at 7 p.m. When I had a concert, I would play them earlier, often confusing people with the change in time. On campus, everyone wanted to know the mystery of the chimes. The enigma was far from complicated. In a small room in the basement of Bryan Hall, on a two-octave keyboard, I played simple melodies that came out, bell-like, from the tower of the building. A few students believed someone pulled down on ropes tied to actual bells to create the sound.

After Bonnie and Jan left, I guided my sisters to the Stouts' bedroom. They wanted to talk some more and mentioned a few youngsters my age and younger whose parents were desperate to get them out of Cuba. "This is enough for tonight," I said. My sisters' stories had pierced my flesh like arrows, and the resulting wounds were still bleeding as I kissed Betty, then Tere goodnight. I needed the emotional hemorrhage to stop before I could hear any more of their or my parents' travails. Or anybody else's.

The apartment had everything we needed and we were grateful for that, but my sisters, understandably, were bored. They spoke rudimentary English and had no friends, other than Bonnie. Through her, they found part-time jobs cleaning sororities but my sisters felt uncomfortable befriending any of the girls. They saw themselves as hired help. Not equals.

Tere became abrasive if she perceived any kind of threat to the bond that united us as siblings. And to her Bonnie was a threat. When Bonnie offered rides to church, Tere turned them down. She preferred to walk. When Bonnie came with gifts of groceries or clothes, she accepted with a grin. Fidel would have been more likely to smile at the U.S. than Tere to show appreciation. She trusted no one.

Betty, my twin, my preferred dance partner, showed a side I had ignored before. The distance between us over the last couple of years had provided a different lens through which I could now view her. The glaze on the beautiful china doll had worn off, the porcelain itself, chipped. Although her looks and charm could still melt hearts, I felt she often used them as manipulative tools. She had no intention of marrying Antonio, the young man she was engaged to in Cuba. "I never loved him...after Reinaldo, I never loved anyone." She met Reinaldo when she was an impressionable fifteen-year old. And after he left her for an older woman, she felt she could never open her heart to anyone else.

Antonio, who had gone to Havana to bid a tearful farewell to her, did not know that once Betty's plane entered Mexican skies, *mamá* would return the engagement ring, a diamond that had belonged to his late mother.

Something of a similar ilk apparently happened in Mexico. After Tere and *tía* Chuchi left for Miami, a lonely Betty found consolation in a young man who lived near her. They declared their undying love to each other, but, once in Pullman, she would not accept his calls. "He was an *entretenimento*," she said.

In our younger years she was the sun I would point to with pride when I introduced her as "my twin." That sun now reveled in shadows. She objected to my spending so much time at school practicing or with friends: Bonnie, Linda, the Stouts. "You leave Tere and me home making love to a TV we don't understand." She was right, but, unlike Tere, she could offer a smile that was the picture of gratitude, and love, to anyone I introduced her to.

I could understand their boredom. I was gone most of the time, making the twenty-minute trek to and from campus four times a day. In the morning to classes; back for dinner (Tere became the cook and turned into a soup specialist of sorts); then, up the hill again to practice, and back when it was almost time for bed.

Every night, while my sisters slept their boredom away, I'd follow the same ritual. From a second-hand record player I had bought from another student, which I had placed on the floor next to my bed, I would listen to Barber's *Adagio for String*, its melody a cry of longing that moved forward in cathartic steps. At the end, after a sigh, I would play one of Joan Sutherland's recordings of Bel Canto arias. The purity of her tone inspired me. To me, if flowers could sing, they'd sound like Sutherland. After a few arias, I'd stop the record, turn down the cover, get under it and go to sleep. I'd dream of imitating the purity of Sutherland's singing in my own playing and a future filled with joy and music. This nightly ritual put a stop to the nightmares about *papá*, although he and *mamá* would still endure challenges I could not even imagine yet.

Chapter Twenty-One

IF MY sisters' time in Mexico tested their survival skills, my parents' was filled with enough drama to qualify as a *telenovela,* one of those soap operas popular with Latin-American audiences.

Mamá and *papá* arrived in Mexico the first week of February, 1965. Because *mamá* was born in Spain, although she had a Cuban passport, Mexico considered her a Spanish citizen and required a deposit of eight hundred dollars—some sort of bond that applied to immigrants from countries other than Cuba. We had wired the money in advance to the American Embassy; as proof, we sent a photocopy of the wire to a friend from Antilla who was already in Mexico with his family, waiting to enter the United States. He had agreed to meet my parents at the airport. Immigration authorities, however, would not accept the photocopy, and kept *mamá* in detention while *papá* went to the American Embassy to retrieve the money. We had wired a total of nine hundred dollars, enough for *mamá*'s deposit and an extra one hundred so they could get by the first few days in the Mexican capital. We assumed *el Refugio* would help them afterwards.

At the Embassy, an officer told them they had returned the money because my parents were not American citizens. At his friend's suggestion, *papá* called a lawyer, not the one who tried to take advantage of Betty, but someone the friend knew who was familiar with Cuban immigration issues in Mexico. *Papá* explained the situation, and the lawyer promised to resolve the matter by the end of the day.

Papá and his friend went back to the airport to check on *mamá*. After making sure she was fine (although according to how *papá* told it later, "she was sobbing and shaking with fear"), they went back to the city, this time to *Gobernación*, a place my sisters knew well. Concerned the lawyer might not solve the problem by the end of the day, *papá's* friend had suggested they take matters into their own hands.

At *Gobernación*, they encountered about one hundred Cubans waiting for their turn to be seen. By then, the issue with *mamá* had so unhinged him, *papá's* voice failed him. *Papá's* friend explained the situation, and they were allowed to get to the front of the line. The official they spoke to knew of the case—the lawyer had already contacted him—and *papá* received the necessary clearance to get *mamá* out of immigration. *Papá* had to leave his passport with the official and was given an appointment at *Gobernación* for the following morning.

Before going back to the airport, they stopped at a modest hotel to reserve a room. At first, the person in charge was reluctant to help; *papá* had no money for a deposit and no form of identification. *Papá* found his voice, explained the problem, and secured a room for one hundred and twenty dollars a month that included breakfast and lunch.

He and *mamá* arrived at the hotel around eight thirty that evening; soon thereafter, they called us collect. *Papá* was first to speak. He told us about their struggles. I explained we had received the money back from the Embassy that very same day and had wired it back immediately to the main branch of the *Banco Nacional de Méjico*. They were already in transit and we couldn't contact them to alert them of the new development.

When *mamá* took the phone, she forced herself to say. "Can't wait to be reunited with you. That's all I ask. Whatever we endure is what God wants...but as long as we finally get back... together... as a family." As I heard her trembling voice, my eyes watered. Betty and Tere wanted to speak. I handed the receiver to Tere, who was closest to me, but kept my ear next to the phone so I could hear the other side of the conversation. At one point, I overheard *mamá* say, "We have to hang up. This is going to cost you a fortune." Before she put the receiver down, I heard her warn *papá*: "Lorenzo, be careful... that box spring is held up by bricks."

We went to bed relieved the issue of the money was resolved. The following day, however, we received another collect call. I wasn't home so Betty accepted it. "*Papá* is desperate," she told me that evening. "He went to the bank and they said they didn't have the money."

The following morning, I called the bank, but after reciting the number, date and time of the wire, my pleas went nowhere. I spoke to a Sánchez, a Menéndez, a Baéz. They all said, "The money is not here." The words bespoke problems.

What next?

On the days that followed, I made many more calls to the *Banco Nacional* and to Western Union, the company we had used to wire the money. *Papá* also paid daily visits to the bank. Throughout, the bank insisted it did not have the money.

At last, on April 9th, nineteen days after we had wired it, the money surfaced. "It's been here all the time," an employee told *papá* during one of his many visits to the bank. "It went to the wrong department."

What we learned from the experience was not to send anything to the American Embassy that did not involve

American citizens, and not to trust the *Banco Nacional de Méjico*. Was the confusion at the bank due to inefficiency, bureaucracy, or plain corruption? Who knows?

The Mexican sun brightened for my parents, and five months after their arrival in the Aztec capital, they received their American visas and entered the United States, staying in Miami with *tía* Chuchi for a few days. Then, on July 7th, 1965, a year after my sisters' arrival in Pullman, they flew to Spokane, an hour or so from Pullman. Betty and I went with Bonnie to meet their flight; Tere stayed home, because, although Bonnie had borrowed her husband's car, there was not enough room for everyone. Beni was absent. His excuse? A baseball tournament.

The days leading up to my parents' arrival filled me with trepidation.

It had been a while since we lived under the same roof on *Calle Miramar* in Antilla. Since I arrived in this country as a senior in high school, we had communicated only via letters, postcards and the occasional phone call. I was now a junior at WSU, a time when most college students look forward to becoming independent from their parents. This was the American way. In Cuba, however, children lived with their parents until they married, and then they'd move next door or down the block. I believed this was what my parents expected.

What would it be like to live with them here?

It would be different.

We could hug them before going to classes and when we returned home for dinner.

But...

It would be different.

We could kiss them goodnight. Every night.

But…
It would be different.
They were our parents.
We, no longer children.

When my parents' plane landed and people exploded out of the assigned gate, my eyes scanned the crowd. I recognized no one. Had they missed their plane or had I forgotten what they looked like? Then I heard a familiar voice, "Loren, *mi vida.*" It was *mamá*. I looked at her. Her skin did not glow the way I remembered; her eyes had lost their vitality as well. Her dress seemed a size or two too big. Later I learned the dress came from *el Refugio*, the only help they received, unlike the support, although meager, this organization gave my sisters while in Mexico. *Papá* wore a brown suit that drooped from the shoulders, like melted chocolate. It was the same suit he brought from Cuba, which he wore day after day in Mexico and now looked as tired as he was. His black hair had turned white, giving his head the look of a snow-covered mountain. These were the same parents I had said goodbye to at the Havana airport in 1962. Yet, they were different. Time had infected them with the virus of aging; and although they expressed happiness at our reunion, underneath their demeanor, a certain sadness peeked through, a melancholy often seen in old people who can't let go of the past.

I was first to hug *mamá*. Her tight embrace almost stopped my breathing. Through sobs, she managed to say, "Please, please, promise we'll never be separated again." Her statement unsettled me; after all the separation was never my idea. In some ways I understood. It was not me she was talking to, but fate, God, as if by saying the words aloud, she could stop the episode from repeating itself.

Papá approached Betty; both cried into an embrace. After a few seconds, he let go of her and turned to me. "Loren, you're so grown up."

I was not sure I had changed physically that much—well, my hair was thinning out a bit. Inside, I was a different person, though: independent, resourceful. Finding imaginative, practical solutions to life's challenges was the resolve of all *Pedro Pans*. It was engraved on our brains the day we left Cuba. We stood up to challenges and turned promises into potentials, potentials into hope and hope into reality. I hadn't done it alone, though. I had Linda to thank for my music, and Bonnie for making it possible for my sisters and parents to be here. So, yes, I was a different person.

When *papá* hugged me, I buried myself in his chest. His breathing echoed my rapid heartbeat. *Papá* loathed showing his emotions in public. In fact, the last time I remembered such public display was at the airport in Havana the day Beni and I left. When he released me from his tearful embrace, he turned to Bonnie. "You must be Bonnie. Thank you. Thank you for taking care of our children. I don't know how we could ever repay you." He hugged Bonnie, whose eyes matched the red of her lipstick.

She planted a kiss on *papá's* cheek, leaving a red mark, which she quickly wiped off with her fingers. She gave *mamá* a kiss next.

"Are you ready?" Bonnie asked, her chin pointing to the sign "Baggage Claim."

Oh, yes, we were ready to retrieve the luggage and proceed with an experience that had stayed in the text of the unrealized for too long. Political conflicts beyond our control had wedged a chasm between our lives, our realities. Ours here, theirs, so far away. But now their physical presence was an unmistakable truth. I was a proud *Pedro Pan*. I had reunited my family.

By then, my sisters were no longer cleaning sororities. Betty had obtained a position as a dark-room assistant in a photography studio, and Tere a job as an office clerk at the student bookstore on campus. I was teaching piano to non-music majors and accompanying recitals for which I was paid; although three hundred dollars per concert, approximately a concert a month, did not go too far. It was enough, though, to have helped my parents while they stayed in Mexico.

At last we could say, *adiós* Mexico, *adiós* El Refugio. *Mamá* and *papá* are here. And we can help them.

Part of our help came in the shape of a new place, one no longer a gift from the Catholic Church. The house, right on campus, on Avenue B, faced a fraternity and was sandwiched between a sorority on the left and student housing on the right; our old apartment was being demolished to give way to a new building.

Betty, Tere, and I had painted the apartment ourselves while Beni remained in Richland. "Someday, he'd surface," I'd say, pretending indifference, although I resented his absence. We seemed to have lost him to baseball fields, from which he heard the cheer of spectators from the bleachers but not his family's clamor for his presence.

Bonnie parked in front of the apartment, and from the driver's seat, kissed everyone good night. She gave us time to take the suitcases out of the trunk. I took one piece, *papá* the other. As Bonnie's car disappeared down the hill on Avenue B, our front door opened, letting out a stream of light. Then, the figure of Tere, already dressed in soft pink pajamas, appeared. With circular hand motions, she propelled herself toward us.

"Ay, *mami, mami, papi, papi,*" she kept saying, kissing and hugging one, then the other; she would touch each on the arm, the face, going back and forth between *mamá* and *papá,* as if to make sure they were real.

It was a clear night that sang of hope and new beginnings; the moon watched us as we took the steps up to the porch, where chains suspended from the ceiling held a swing typical of houses in the South. Once on the porch, *mamá* and *papá* looked around to familiarize themselves with the new surroundings. When the swing's physical presence registered on *mamá*'s consciousness, she rushed toward it and plopped herself down. "*Ay, qué rico.* Such pleasure," she said, dropping her head back to allow the soft summer breeze to kiss her face. That simple act seemed to have given her back some of the youth she had lost; I had to coax her to get up. When she did, we went in, and walked through the house.

"This is a palace," *papá* said.

"*Ay, si,*" *mamá* said.

Once we finished touring the house, we sat in the living room: *mamá* and *papá* on the couch; Betty, Tere and I on the floor facing them. We talked the night away, reminiscing about friends and relatives still in Cuba, and of times when we were still children.

"My happiest times were when you were all little and I'd put you all to bed," *mamá* said.

"Yes, at five in the afternoon," I said.

"Always a trouble maker...telling your brother and sisters."

"You'd close the shutters, and tell us it was night out. We could hear kids playing outside."

"I wanted your *papi* to come home to a quiet house."

As she spoke, I had a sense she still saw us as her children. I tried to erase the thought from my mind.

"*Bueno,*" papá said, yawning his way up from the sofa. "We must leave something for tomorrow."

"*Ay, mi Loren, mi Loren, que gusto me da verte...tan buen mozo.* And Tere and Betty...the three of you together," mamá said. "Beni's the only one missing."

Before she joined *papá,* I handed *mamá* a scrapbook I had placed under the sofa. It contained programs from my concerts, drawings I'd made in art classes, letters I'd received from them and photographs of Beni and me in Miami, plus pictures of Linda, Chuck, and others. "You can look at it tomorrow."

"*El major regalo.* The best gift," mamá said.

After kissing both *mamá* and *papá* goodnight, I uttered a silent prayer of thanks. We were together at last. *Mamá* was right. Beni was the only one missing.

Chapter Twenty-Two

SEPTEMBER WINDS whispered the beginning of the fall semester. My parents had been in Pullman a little over two months and were looking forward to the turning of the leaves, though not the teeth-shattering weather they expected winter to bring.

I was on stage in the concert hall of the new music building, practicing Brahms' *Intermezzo in E-flat minor*, a composition that some have described as a tone poem to mourning. From the Steinway Grand, my fingers evoked the fragile melody, followed by the hushed, mysterious rumble of the left hand. A few measures later, I had the eerie feeling someone was in the hall, listening, watching. I looked to my right, my fingers still lingering over the Brahms, and noticed a lone figure in the back of the auditorium, leaning on the doorframe. My head jerked, a common reaction when so immersed in something we tune out everything around us and are surprised by the sudden presence of someone. She stood there for a few seconds; then stepped forward, swaying down the aisle in heels that well knew their role of parading her in front of others. Her smile went off like flashbulbs at a Hollywood premiere.

The melody of the *Intermezzo* hung in mid-air, like the feet of a child playing on the overhead parallel bars.

When she reached the edge of the stage, she tapped on the light oak parquet floor as if to say, "Here I am, now what?"

I walked downstage, crouched in front of her, and, lost in the creamy brown of her eyes, said, "You certainly are a pretty one."

My words poured out of me before I could stop them.

She tilted her head, feigning embarrassment, and her face took on a mask meant to convey she didn't deserve the compliment. She knew I knew she knew she was beautiful; although behind her confidence, hid vulnerability, a trait, perhaps, not many had noticed. I stared for the longest time, trying to unravel the riddle of this master painting come to life, probably hoping to figure out why such feelings of curiosity and sexual desire were stirring inside me. Was I, subconsciously, wanting to live up to my parents' expectations for me?

"I think I'm going to like you," she said.

"Don't. I can be trouble."

"Care to explain?"

I was not about to elaborate; I was not sure what I meant, anyway. Everything and perhaps nothing at all.

"By the way, I'm Carole."

She need not have told me; I knew exactly who she was. The sister of someone whose senior recital I had accompanied the semester before, she had just entered WSU as a freshman and was going to major in voice. I had spoken to her on the phone and had agreed to play for her—her brother had recommended me. I didn't know much about her other than her placing in the finals of the Miss Washington contest. When I agreed to play for her audition for the student production of *Guys and Dolls* and voice lessons, I assumed I would encounter another pretty girl with mediocre talent.

I was wrong on both counts. She possessed beauty, the likes of which were seldom seen outside the movies, and a singing talent, I was about to discover, that was far from pedestrian.

I looked at my watch. How could I have forgotten? I was supposed to have been looking for her.

"No, no, I'm early...someone mentioned you were here. I thought I'd find you. Easier than your going from room to room looking for me."

She didn't need to worry. I would have found her anywhere, although the description she gave me on the phone could have applied to just about anyone. "Light brown hair that comes down almost to my shoulders."

"How's your brother?" I asked, trying to make idle conversation.

"Fine. Fine. He says hello."

Her rendition of Mozart's *Vedrai Carino* offered a delightful cure for love; the Strauss' "Laughing Song" from *Die Fledermaus* suggested worldly charms that seemed unusual in someone so young; and "If I Were a Bell," one of Sarah's solos from *Guys and Dolls,* professed drunkenness as an excuse for making love.

By the time we were finished, *I* was drunk with desire for her. So much so that I couldn't bring myself to end a practice session that, if the gods were fair, should have lasted forever. It was Carole who brought it to a close saying she had to go to class. She gathered her music, walked to the door, then she turned around. "That went well...good chemistry," she said. I took a few steps toward her, cupped her chin with my right hand, tilted her head up, and kissed lips that were soft and as warm as the sun itself.

When I introduced Carole to my parents, who by then had already spent a summer in Pullman, she charmed them. Most of my schoolmates begrudged her. They felt that since meeting Carole, I was ignoring my own practicing.

During the school year, Carole and I became inseparable—our bodies often entwined by their own music and voicing discord when they had to separate. I even joined the chorus of *Guys and Dolls*. The year before, I had joined the cast of *West Side Story*, playing the role of Chino, which got me a notice in the Spokane paper: "Lorenzo Martínez was a *smoldering* Chino." At the time, I didn't know what the word meant. I had enjoyed performing in that production and thought that *Guys and Dolls* with Carole and I in it would turn into an experience just as *smoldering*.

Our relationship, however, hit a snag before the end of the school year. She wanted to date others while home for the summer. The request made no sense. I had taken my cue from my parents. They'd had a courtship of nine years. My mother's father refused to allow her to marry *papá*, a "nobody," according to him. But, steadfast in their feelings for each other, *mamá* and *papá* refused to give in and withstood a series of awkward incidents, such as when chaperoned by *mamá's* mother, *abuela* Lola, they would take in a movie and *abuelo* would show up at the theatre, grabbing *mamá* by the arm to take her home. There were not many places in Antilla where they could hide. If *mamá* and *papá* had lasted nine years—until she threatened to elope—why was it so difficult for Carole and I to continue our loyalty over a summer? Her proposal seemed too modern and American for my taste. When I told Beni about it, he had a strong reaction. "She wants to be a slut."

My opinion differed. Away from Carole, I questioned my loyalty to her, and old feelings crowded my mind. Was I using Carole to veil a reality that would never go away?

Today I wouldn't have put either one of us through such a test. At the time, though, I reveled in a role my parents applauded me for; *mamá* in particular was headstrong about my marrying Carole.

When Carole went home, I buried myself in summer school activities and hoped the warm weather would lift my mood as well as *mamá's*. She'd had a difficult time since arriving in Pullman. The grey skies and cold weather had affected her spirits. She lived on Valium, her emotions flattened out by the medication.

Even when she claimed, "I'm so happy to be here with my children," which she said to friends when they visited, the words had no resonance. They were as leveled as a sea at rest.

Papá adjusted more easily. Days after their arrival in Pullman, he accepted a job washing pots and pans in the kitchen of one of the dorms on campus. A man who barely knew what went on in a kitchen had accepted his fate—even when his hands bled from scrubbing the stubbornly stained pots. "I'm grateful to this country. I'll do whatever I need to do."

At first, *mamá* took a job cleaning sororities as my sisters had, but this lasted only until *papá* accepted a position as an accountant in the School of Veterinary. "You don't have to work any more," he told her.

I was not sure that was a good idea. Her being home alone during the day contributed to her sense of isolation and overall depression. To compensate, she embraced the maternal role as if possessed. She worked nonstop: cooking, washing dishes, doing laundry, ironing, keeping track of our whereabouts. My sisters were pleased to have *mamá* fuss over them.

Beni, who had joined us on a work/study program the fall after my parents arrived, accepted the new rules with no hint of rebellion. He worked part-time in the library, and although he took his job seriously, he seemed less committed to school, often skipping classes or studying only enough to pass a test. He enjoyed *mamá's* Cuban cooking, and she made his favorite, sweet plantains, sometimes as a study bribe. "Here, here, to help you study."

After a sarcastic *"¡Si, si, como no!* Sure, sure," he'd walk away. Of course, he'd come back to eat the plantains.

I was, by far, the most rebellious of the siblings, particularly toward *mamá*. I was already juggling the demands of two other mother figures: Bonnie, who, I believe, wanted me to show more interest in her daughter Jan; and Linda, who expected me to spend holidays with her family rather than my own. Adding *mamá* to that mix made me feel like a V-shaped chicken bone whose ends were being pulled not in two but three opposite directions. At least, Bonnie and Linda didn't treat me as a child.

Before my parents arrived in Pullman, I had asked myself what it would be like to live with them again. My response turned out to be prophetic.

It would be different.

One Friday night, I borrowed our family car, an old beat-up brown Buick we had purchased from an ad in the local paper, and drove some classmates over to Moscow, Idaho, a few miles from Pullman. Although I seldom drank, with Carole gone for the summer, I decided a night of fun and beer would do me good.

At the bar, one of my friends, also a music student, sat at a piano stuck in a dark corner and started playing

Gymnnopédie, a suite by avant-garde French composer Erik Satie. The dissonant harmonies prompted the manager to ask him to "stop banging on the piano." We howled with laughter, particularly after my friend, without missing a beat, modulated into "Lara's theme" from *Dr. Zhivago,* a film playing in theaters then. When we left the place, we drove back to Pullman and continued drinking at one of our classmate's apartments, our riotous banter waking up his two roommates. By the time I got home, it was past three in the morning.

When I entered, a figure jumped at me from the dark. It was *mamá.* "Do you know what time it is? I was going to ask *papi* to call the police." Her anxiety could not have shaken the moment more.

"*Mamá,* if you want to stay up and wait for me, that's fine. But, I'm not keeping to *your* curfew." My voice matched hers in loudness.

"I was worried to death."

"I'm sorry," I said, my tone sarcastic.

"This is how you pay me back…after all I do for you?"

"*Mamá,* you brought me into this world, and sent me here, to become a man, a free man, and not remain a child forever," I said. "You can't put me to bed at five in the afternoon and tell me it's night already." The words blurred around the edges.

Suddenly, the overhead light came on. I covered my eyes. *Papá* had entered the room. "Why are you talking to your *mami* that way?" As I struggled to keep steady on my feet, he asked, "Have you been drinking?"

"A little. So?" I couldn't remember expressing such defiance since our confrontation in Antilla about the telegram. No time for apologies, though. I had to make a quick exit before I puked all over myself or the carpet. Without another word, I left them there, stunned, and waddled my way to my room.

In the dark, I climbed up to my bunk, hoping not to disturb Beni. The bed spun around like an-out-of-control carrousel. I held onto the handrails for dear life. Sweat poured out of me; I vowed I'd never drink again!

My senior year at WSU began, and as casually as if we were just putting our beachwear away, Carole and I put the summer behind us. We resumed our relationship. But it would never be the same. The intensity of our interactions lightened as our suntans faded.

That year, I accompanied one concert after another, including Becky's senior recital, which featured Rodrigo's *De los Álamos Vengo*, a piece of subtle lyricism that offered me a nostalgic reminder of the *álamos* in Antilla. Hailing from Seattle, Becky was a trusted friend with whom I shared many classes; her scholastic achievements (straight A's) matched her impressive vocal talent. Because she also played the piano, she understood the role of the pianist not as a mere accompanist but equal partner; performing with her was pure joy.

For my own recital, I chose Beethoven's *Thirty Two Variations in C minor*, a composition whose complex changes of mood and tempo Raúl had successfully brought to life many times at *abuela's* apartment. My recital went well and it was followed with a tempting offer: a fellowship to pursue my master's at WSU. Besides free tuition, I would receive a salary of twelve thousand dollars a year, an amount that at the time seemed princely. In exchange, I would teach piano to non-music majors.

The downside was my parents' view of me as still a child, which burned inside me like a hot iron. I believed their opinion would not waver over the next couple of years if I stayed at WSU.

Pulling me in another direction was the fact that many of my friends were planning to further their education elsewhere.

Becky would go to the New England Conservatory, where a couple of music students who graduated from WSU the year before were already pursuing advanced degrees. Other students would go to Indiana. Barrett Stout had left for New York and had enrolled at the New School for Social Research to continue his studies in philosophy. He offered to share his apartment if I decided to forego my fellowship and come to New York. "It's in the East Village…on East Eleventh between Avenues C and D…got a bathtub in the kitchen… you get used to it."

The more I heard about others' plans to study elsewhere, the more the temptation and the greater the conflict. How could I leave my parents now? Even the thought felt like a betrayal. Yet, two weeks before school started, something snapped inside me, like button on a shirt that was too tight; I made a decision.

Beni drove us to Spokane in our new Chevrolet, a dark beige vehicle that Betty had already scratched on the side when pulling out of the narrow driveway between our house and the sorority next door. Beni had missed our sisters' and parents' arrivals, yet he was willing to see me off. Maybe driving the new car had something to do with it.

At the airport, the mood was unlike the one hovering over our family the day Beni and I flew to Miami. Smiles covered our faces, as we reserved the tears, and they were quiet ones, for the end. Besides, there had been plenty of waterworks already, particularly from *mamá*, when I told her of my plans. Although she claimed to understand, she said, "You're abandoning us. We came here to be together. We'll follow you." *Oh, no, you won't.*

Papá had a different reaction. He questioned my feelings for Carole, and when I said I was not planning to marry her after all, he said I was "going through a phase." I didn't ask him to elaborate.

Carole had accompanied us, and she and I had our pictures taken in a photo booth that stood at the end of one of the corridors. Our poses ended with a passionate kiss, our love recorded for posterity. Although I wanted to believe something different, I knew deep inside I would never see her again. The pictures, which I took with me, would be the ashes of our love. It was over and she knew it. I felt a sense of nostalgia. We'd had fun together. She had actually given me self-confidence and helped me believe that for a moment I could be happy with her.

Boarding time came, and Carole and I kissed again. Beni winked at me. I guessed he didn't realize Carole and I were over. After kissing *mamá*, I went up to *papá*, looked him in the eye and said, "*Gracias…I want to say… gracias."* I knew these were words he had wanted to hear from me for a long time.

When I left Cuba, my core had lost its music, and it took a while before I heard the rumblings of a melody wanting to come through. When it emerged, it came with lyrics written for me. Now, I wanted to write my own, to be the composer of my own future.

I felt optimistic. I was a *Pedro Pan*, after all. If I had done it once, thanks to the generous hearts of many people, there was no reason success would escape me a second time. America was forgiving. At the beginning, I had looked at it with resentment, yet the country accepted me and my parents, providing opportunities for us as immigrants that were available only in a land I now loved and proudly called my own.

When I landed at LaGuardia Airport, there was no *Padre* to meet me, whether he was late or not, and no Beni to worry about. It was me taking care of my destination; I alone responsible for myself. It felt different. It felt good.

I called out, "Taxi!" My yell pierced the dense New York air.

Once inside the cab, my heart sped to a setting no metronome could track. I directed the driver, "Eleventh Street and Avenue D." Somehow, as I said those words, a sense of belonging washed over me.

Chapter Twenty-Three

NEW YORK CITY offered a memorable welcome, the kind that makes you want to pack your bags and return home. It was a week after my arrival. Taking in the electric energy of the neighborhood, I walked north on Second Avenue. Buildings facing west glowed from the morning sun; people crowded the sidewalks; youngsters on their way to school skidded toward and away from me while yelling for their friends; car horns tooted nonstop. Before I reached 13th street, someone approached me from behind, pushing something I assumed was a weapon against my ribs. "Keep on walking and don't say a word." The accent was Hispanic. I froze. "Keep walking. Told ya. And don't turn around." At that moment someone else jumped in front of me, demanding I hand over my watch. The first guy kept pressing his weapon against my ribs while the one in front, dark skin, his eyes full of scorn, slid the watch off my wrist with the skills of a magician (*"See this watch? Gone!"*).

The incident transported me back to the scene at the Havana airport. I couldn't believe the watch I had bought to replace the one taken from me then had just been stolen. People passed us on both sides. No one aware of what was happening. I felt like screaming, but whatever was bobbing up and down my ribs gagged my thoughts. Barrett, my new roommate, had mentioned that a week before I moved into the neighborhood, someone was killed only yards from our building.

It took intense concentration not to burst into tears once I reached the Manhattan School of Music. Even the sight of Josephine Whitford, dean of students, a woman who reminded me of *abuela,* and whose smile twinkled along with her eyes, failed to lift my gloom. I mentioned nothing of what had just happened.

I had visited the school a few times already. Because the semester was in progress and the school was no longer holding auditions, my being admitted as a student had seemed unlikely. But Dr. Bailey called someone he knew, and based on his recommendation I was accepted "on probation." If I did well, I would be considered a regular student, starting the following semester.

My conditional status notwithstanding, I received a student loan that paid for part of my tuition and obtained a part-time job teaching piano in a private music academy in New Jersey, mostly to children who hated taking lessons. Despite the loan, the job, and cheap rent, less than thirty dollar a month for my half, I struggled to cover the rest of my tuition and personal expenses. I was back to my Matecumbe days, penniless, in a city I found gray, dirty and intimidating, not to mention dangerous.

A second mugging followed the first by only a week. I walked up the zigzag of stairs to our walk-up apartment. When I turned left on the third floor landing, someone intercepted my steps. I recognized him as the guy who had yielded the weapon during the first mugging. This time he was flashing a knife. "Help!" My cry echoed through the hall. I was done with being afraid of this *hijo de puta.* "Look, I don't want to hurt you. Give me your money," he said. I kept shaking my head, hoping for someone to come to my rescue. No door opened. I thought about running back down and out of the building but realized that he would be inside waiting for me when I returned. I ended up giving him the ten dollars and change I had in my pocket.

After that, I flew in and out of the apartment propelled by fear. Once I returned home, around four or five in the afternoon, I stayed in. Nights often found me standing in front of the living room window, which opened to a courtyard, staring at the moon—the only other window was in the kitchen and looked onto a brick wall. The moon kept its vigil, concerned, protective, yet gave no indication it would shield me from harm.

In letters to and phone conversations with my parents, I painted a different picture. "Everything is great. I love being here." It reminded me of my withholding from them the reality of exile while they were still in Cuba, the bad *becas*, our difficult life with the Tudors. But New York was different. Coming here was my decision. I couldn't admit to having made a mistake, particularly in light of *mamá's* constant messages. "*Mi vida, ¿por qué no regresas? Aquí yo te atiendo. ¿Estás comiendo bien?*" (Why don't you come back? I can take care of you. Are you eating well?)

Even when I talked to Carole, Linda or Mrs. Peterson, I refrained from talking about the muggings or how difficult I found New York. I mentioned my loneliness but nothing else. As far as they were concerned I was doing what I wanted and was happy. True, I was doing what I wanted. But happy was a different story.

My spirits were revived by a telephone call from Becky, my WSU classmate now at the New England Conservatory. "I'm planning to come to New York," she said. "Can I stay with you?" Of course! She could have my bed; I'd take the floor. I warned her about the neighborhood, but she didn't seem to mind. As soon as she arrived, she announced she was here for an abortion. My eyes narrowed, not out of disapproval but because I hadn't known this was the reason for her visit. These were the days before Roe vs. Wade. The abortion took place somewhere in New Jersey. I have no recollection where exactly, for I was numbed throughout the experience. I was asked to drop her off at a street corner and wait for her in a nearby bar, where she would join me after the procedure was over. While I waited, I felt as if someone was pounding on my head with a hammer. My fingers felt colder than the beer I held in my hand. I could barely drink from it; my throat had closed. I had no clue where she was. All I knew was the corner where I had dropped her off. Every time the door to the bar opened, I jumped out of my seat. What would I do if anything happened to her? What would I say to her parents? I had met them a few times; her father was a minister. Abortion was so common in Cuba—*la doctora,* who lived next to *abuela,* performed them; *mamá* had used her services a couple of times—that I hadn't allowed myself to think about the practices and consequences of such procedures in this country. Until that moment.

When the bar's door swung open and Becky appeared, her teeth chattered, her hands trembled as she rubbed her stomach in an effort to ease the pain she couldn't erase from her face. I rushed toward her, a sour taste, and not from the beer, had settled in my mouth. Next day, a pale Becky, still shaking, still in pain, flew back to Boston; she never talked about the experience. I respected her silence. I did hear from mutual friends that she'd had a difficult semester because of health issues, which I assumed were related to the abortion.

The experience remained fixed in my mind. Years later, as I advocated and raised funds for programs in Latin America and the Caribbean that promoted the practice of safe sex, I would think of Becky. These programs aimed at avoiding unwanted pregnancies that might result in unsafe abortions.

A month after Becky's visit, I came close to calling my New York game over. My roommate Barrett and I had been out. When we returned, we noticed someone had broken into the vacant apartment next door and made a hole on the wall adjacent to our place. Our apartment was ransacked: drawers emptied out, clothes strewn everywhere. We discovered Barrett's stereo system missing, as well as a locked suitcase I kept under my bed because I had no place to put its contents, a winter coat among other clothes, in my tiny closet. I assumed the burglars didn't want the clothes but had no time to break the lock and decided to take the suitcase in case it held something valuable.

The following day, I saw Dean Whitford, who immediately sensed something was wrong. "Dearie, why are you looking so sad?" I didn't know if she used *dearie* because she couldn't remember the names of the hundreds of students who entered the school every year. Whatever the reason, from her, the term sounded warm.

"I don't know why I'm here," I told her.

"Because it's a good school."

"I don't mean that. New York, I mean."

She adjusted the colorful shawl she often wore, and then pushed the bridge of her glasses up, as if to get a better look at me.

"Well, tell me why," she said.

I hadn't told anyone, including Barrett, any of this, but somehow Dean Whitford generated confidence. "I had lost my music once, then got it back. I walked away from it. From my family. I wanted freedom, I guess."

"Sooner or later, everyone walks away from family."

"Not if you're Cuban," I said, guilt clouding my vision.

She gave me a puzzled look. "Do you want to talk to a counselor?"

I shook my head. I didn't need a counselor. I wasn't crazy. If I had survived the Tudors and conquered Pullman, why would I allow New York to swallow me up in a sea of intimidation? Although I felt violated, I would not allow my spirits to be broken. I was a *Pedro Pan,* and if there was one lesson I had learned from the experience it was to part the curtains to adversity and walk through them with a victorious smile. I'd show my parents and Carole that coming to New York was the right choice. Besides, I couldn't disappoint *abuela.* "You're going to study in New York, just like Raúl. Imagine when he finds out."

During my senior year at WSU, *abuela, tía* Chuchi and *tía* Nena had lived with us. Our small three-bedroom home had stretched like jersey fabric to accommodate them. *Abuela* slept on a pullout sofa in the living room, which I, Beni, or *papá* would open for her every night. The two *tías* shared a makeshift, damp room in the basement, separated from the washer and dryer area by curtains *mamá* had made. *Abuela* and *tía* Nena had flown to Miami, joined *tía* Chuchi, and the three of them had trekked to Pullman for a joyous reunion that in the end turned out to be brief. After one cold winter, they decided to return to Miami. I believe *abuela* would have stayed. She had lived through the Cuban war of independence from Spain, heard stories of her ancestors settling in Cuba after escaping the French Revolution, and survived incredible hardships under Fidel. Her indomitable character would have adapted to cold winters.

Abuela and *tia* Nena's entry into the United States was the result of a memorandum of understanding signed in November 1965, between the Johnson administration and Castro's regime. Both governments had agreed to an orderly, systematic airlift of Cubans who wished to immigrate to the United States, replacing an effort in October of the same year that had resulted in chaos. That October, the Cuban government announced that Cubans living in the United States were welcome to pick up relatives in Cuba and designated the port of Camarioca as the point of embarkation. But mayhem ensued, and an out-of-control mass exodus resulted in a number of deaths at sea; Cubans out of desperation had operated unsafe craft to transport their relatives.

The new agreement would avoid such havoc. Cubans with relatives in this country qualified under the new arrangement—this benefited *abuela* and *tía*. Especial priority was given to siblings and parents of children under twenty-one. Fidel's generosity, however, did not extend to boys of military age, sixteen to twenty-six, or people with certain technical expertise or professions. As a result, many families were separated at the airport when one member was not allowed to embark; harrowing decisions had to be made at the last minute regarding whether to stay in Cuba or leave loved ones behind. The two daily flights set up from Havana to Miami then became known as the Freedom Flights.

Through the Freedom Flights, many *Pedro Pan* children, including El Havanero, were reunited with their parents. The reunions were dramatic, particularly for the younger children, who had forgotten their Spanish and had grown so much the parents didn't recognize them. Beyond the physical change, these children had developed resentment toward their parents. Some believed their parents didn't love them because they had sent them away, depriving them of their childhood.

Accepted as a regular student for the second semester, I received a scholarship, which added to my student loan and extra hours of teaching allowed me to move, without a roommate, to a slightly better neighborhood on East 99th Street. At seventy dollars a month, my new apartment, like the old, had a club-foot tub in the kitchen right by the front door. I could take a bath and answer the door at the same time.

I studied with Zenon Fishbein, an Argentinian who had studied in Vienna, Paris, and Rome, a Chopin specialist, heralded by *The New York Times* as "a real talent" after an unusually impressive debut. Other critics had called him "a master of the grand manner," and "A marvelous colorist...A fine pianist indeed." Besides his impressive talent, Zenon offered his students the same warmth and patience I remembered in Raúl.

Feeling safer in my new neighborhood, I took the moon on night journeys that included visits to a gay bar on Manhattan's East side. I can't recall how I learned of the bar's existence. I can't imagine having asked any of my classmates. A stranger on the street? I don't know. All I know is that when you're determined to do something, somehow you find the way.

Wearing a second-hand coat from Goodwill, I blew in with the winter wind, walking past a crowded, smoke-filled bar to a room in the back where music played. Men of all sizes and shapes stood in a perfect circle around a semi-dark dance floor, occasionally staring at each other. No one spoke. No one danced. Pretending I knew what I was doing, I claimed a place in the circle. Seconds later, I felt a tap on my shoulders. "Lorenzo, aren't you going to say hello?" Without realizing it, I had walked past two boys from Matecumbe who were having a drink at the bar. Rolando was long-limbed with a narrow face and pointed chin; Juan Jesús, at least six inches shorter, made up in weight what Rolando lacked. They had gone to the same *beca* in Colorado. After graduating from college, they came to New York and were now sharing an apartment on Horatio Street.

"Oh, my God, oh, my God, oh, my God," I said as my head jerked back.

"You seemed to know your way around," Juan Jesús said.

"My first time."

They didn't believe me. After reconnecting with them, I started to like New York and would have crammed thirty hours into a twenty-four hour day. Besides classes, practice, and free concerts at the school, I attended performances (standing room) at the Metropolitan Opera and the New York City Ballet, spent time at Rolando and Juan Jesús' apartment, and went to gay bars with them.

At the bars, we placed bets on who would be the first to find a *date* for the night. My promiscuity was unbridled. This was the heyday of the Vietnam War and the phrase "Make Love Not War" had turned into a protest of the war and a slogan that endorsed sexual openness and experimentation. The provocative mantra became my salvo, my way of assuaging guilt for a behavior that was unprecedented in me. When I spoke to Carole on the phone, tremor rang in my voice as I held out on my sexual activities. I had come to New York to learn about myself, and going to gay bars and having sex with men was part of my New York education.

The time I spent at the Manhattan School was referred to as the Vietnam period, and some of my *Pedro Pan* friends, who had reached enlistment age, had gone off to serve in the military. This included Leonardo, my bunk mate at Matecumbe. I prayed he'd come back alive. I barely missed recruitment myself. Once I checked off asthma on the questionnaire, I was dismissed. I was never happier about an affliction that had given me many scary moments, often in the winter time, when it tended to flare up.

If the time before graduation focused on the war in Vietnam, the period after revolved around "wedding bells." Rolando and Juan Jesús, my cohorts in gay bar-hopping, got married. They were "heterosexuals, only experimenting." My twin, Betty, also got married. She had met her husband while dating his roommate, a WSU student; when the roommate dropped her, his friend asked her out. With a recent degree in engineering, her new husband accepted a job in the steel industry in Johnstown, Pennsylvania, a city most famous perhaps for its eight major floods. So, to that city, seventy miles east of Pittsburgh, Betty went, leaving two disconsolate parents, in particular *mamá,* who couldn't believe Beni too had been bitten by the marriage bug while he was still a senior in school and had moved out to set up house with his new bride.

The marriage epidemic had spread to Carole as well. She married a football player from WSU, whom she started seeing during my second year in New York. The end of our relationship came with no anger. We had taken different paths. Hers, to the altar, spared me a confrontation that would have become inevitable, mine meandering along without a map to follow. As I had predicted, I never saw her again.

With Beni and Betty gone from Pullman, my parents felt displaced. "This is a college town. It's for young people," *papá* said. "We're coming to New York." They had believed

I would return once I received my degree, and when I told them of my decision to stay, they decided to follow me.

One Saturday morning, around eleven o'clock, *mamá, papá* and Tere arrived. They drove cross-country in the same car Betty had dented and that Beni took me to the Spokane Airport in. They bounced into my apartment, hooting, bumping into each other, and hugging me once, twice, a million times. I helped bring suitcases and boxes in from the car. Their furniture was in storage until they had an address to send it to.

The next few days presented a series of incongruous images: *mamá* and *papá, Tere,* and I sitting on the floor around a low coffee table that held our drinks—I found the table discarded on the streets and had painted it black. We balanced TV dinners on our laps. They were unaccustomed to frozen dinners, but I had lived on them during my school days, and the size of my kitchen was too small to accommodate any serious cooking.

We all slept in the same room: *mamá* and *papá* squeezing onto my day bed, and Tere and I claiming the floor, using sleeping bags borrowed from my two Matecumbe friends. The casualness if chaotic tone of our interactions was similar to the atmosphere at Matecumbe. Missing were the pine trees, the tents, the dirt road, and other campers. Instead, my parents and Tere experienced a tiny space in a noisy— our collective snoring didn't help—crowded city, with a subway system that helped them get around. *Mamá*'s refusal to get on a train without *papá* would turn into a phobia that lasted for years.

During the two weeks they stayed with me, *mamá* tried to take over. She insisted on cleaning, rearranging my closet, moving furniture around, washing dishes—although there were not many because I had put my foot down when it came to cooking.

I helped Tere go through the classifieds and circled a few ads that looked promising. At her first interview, she was hired on the spot to work in the benefits department of Bankers Trust.

Meanwhile, through someone who had worked for him in Antilla, *papá* heard of an available space in East Flatbush.

Their new one bedroom forced Tere to sleep on a pull-out sofa in the living room. Despite the tight accommodations, *mamá* insisted I move in with them. "We'll get another sofa. It can go right there," she'd say with a smile that glowed like a neon sign as she pointed to the wall opposite the pull-out sofa." When she realized I wasn't budging, her smile would vanish, her eyes would plead, and with a hand over her heart, possibly to show me a love that in her mind I was ignoring, she'd add, "I can cook for you…do your laundry, keep your closet organized."

"Are you out of your mind?"

She thought *me* crazy for not accepting her offer.

Not long after they moved to Brooklyn, *papá* secured a job as an accountant at a mid-Manhattan location. They were settled, but the euphoria of the first few days in New York had disappeared from *mamá's* face. She went back to her wistful days in Pullman. Her eyes lost their luster, her movements turned slow and robotic. Cuba was always in her thoughts: her mother, her sister, whom she "had abandoned" and felt she'd "never see again." The darker her moods, the more she tried to control those around her. Every day, she chose Tere's work outfits. Every day she brought *papá* coffee in bed, and while he showered she would lay out clothes for him to wear. "Someone told me my enemy dressed me," *papá* would complain. When I'd tell him he had a choice, his eyes would open wide. "But, your *mami...*" No one would go against her. She was *mamá*; the woman who was the "glue to the family"; the woman who had sacrificed for us and deserved "nothing but our love in return." In her eyes, however, the only way I could show my "love" was by moving in with them.

I believed in family ties, but I had come to New York in search of independence, and moving in with them would make me feel as if I were throwing out everything I'd gained. Dean Whitford's words resonated in my mind; "Sooner or later, everyone walks away from family."

Chapter Twenty-Four

SINCE ARRIVING in this country, my life had been one of joy and heartache, happening so close together that at times they seemed like the same feeling. A moment that stands out, because of its unexpected outcome, took place shortly after I came to New York.

One of the young men I had met at a gay bar invited me to his birthday party. Blond, tall and gawky, Bill showed an interest in *dating*. The feeling was not reciprocal. Besides, in my mind then, men with men just had sex. They didn't date. Although reluctantly, I accepted Bill's birthday invitation.

Champagne flowed from the expert hands of a waiter who weaved his way through the crowded living room without spilling a drop. After a few attempts at conversation— it was impossible to hear above the symphonic-like din that played the room—I squeezed onto a yellow sofa next to a woman of undetermined age, who identified herself as Maxine. Then a guy about my age, sparkling brown eyes and streaked blond hair, sat on my lap without asking for permission. He drank from one of those shallow, broad-bowled champagne glasses that according to legend was molded on the breasts of Marie Antoinette.

"Oh, you know Thom," the woman said.

"Never met him before."

"Would you like a drink?" Thom asked.

"No, thanks, I don't drink," I said, trying to sound casual, when in fact I was annoyed he was sitting on my lap. Uninvited.

"The last sip," he said, offering me his glass.

He got up several times for a refill and always came back to offer a "last sip." Several "last sips" later, I'd had a full glass of champagne and he many glasses, enough that he didn't care about showing a marked interest in the birthday boy's *date*.

"You have to see me home," he said, his words barely surfacing behind a cloud of one *Marie Antoinette* too many.

I did take him home. In a large apartment on West 11th Street, a marble fireplace in the living room greeted us. I found the bedroom in the back—it too displayed a marble fireplace. I put him to bed and with some difficulty, I undressed him. I folded his clothes, placed them on a chair nearby, and left.

The following day, he called complaining, "You walked out on me."

"I never said I'd stay."

Our phone conversations continued. Because he worked in television and had to be in the studio by five in the morning, he had a hard time staying awake for chats that took place around ten at night when I got home from teaching or rehearsals. His occasional snoring created exclamations marks that stopped many sentences mid-stream. Despite the *drowsy* conversations, we learned a lot about each other, he of my experience as a *Pedro Pan*, I of his military service and work as a set decorator at CBS, assigned to daytime soaps, specials, and the news.

I resisted his invitations to dinner. "Look, I don't want an affair. We have several friends in common. It's uncomfortable."

"Who said this was an affair? You've heard of forever?"

I wasn't looking to date and let alone for a forever with a man. I thought he was crazy and told him so.

After a month of calls where he'd say yes, and I'd say no, he'd say yes, and I'd say no, I finally consented, and we went out to dinner.

The restaurant, recommended by a CBS colleague, had suffered a power failure earlier that day, something we didn't find out until we started ordering. "No, we don't have it," the waiter said after the first four dishes, his voice an apologetic whisper, his cheeks flushed. "We had to throw out a lot of stuff."

To compensate for the awkward first part of the evening, Thom suggested after-dinner drinks at the Plaza. The romantic grandeur of the Palm Court put us in the mood for a hansom cab ride around Central Park. A line of horse-drawn carriages spread out in front of the hotel. We got into one. No sooner had we turned into the park than a trio of hoodlums started throwing pebbles at us and screaming "faggots, faggots." I took a blanket folded next to me and dove under it while the driver used his whip to stop the boys from jumping onto the carriage. When I was told it was safe, I resurfaced and turned to Thom, "You and your ideas." My voice flogged the night as if I were whipping the horse to get away from that gang of hoodlums and from an experience that reminded me too much of the two muggings and apartment burglary I had experienced in New York at the beginning of my stay. *What a city!*

Two months later, after daily calls where he'd again say yes, and I'd say no, he'd say yes, and I say, no, I moved in with him.

I still thought the idea absurd, but encouraged by my two Matecumbe friends and Bill himself, who had given up on the notion of the two of us as a couple, I figured I'd give it a try.

And when I did, New York found me experiencing intimacy without regret for the first time. I owed this feeling as much to the city as to Thom himself, who insisted and insisted until I allowed myself to walk with him a path that led to self-fulfillment and ultimate freedom. Carole was already married and out of my life.

By then, my parents had been in Brooklyn for about a year. All I said to them initially was that I moved in with a roommate in the Village and that soon they would get a chance to meet him. When they did, and I explained the situation, my mother's response was, "he's my son now. He has to call me *mami.*"

My father too embraced him into the family. Their approval of a part of my life I thought I could never share with them was unexpected and comforting. The reality was that *mamá* and my sisters had questioned my sexuality before, so when confronted with the news they hardly blinked. *Papá,* who thought my going to New York was *just a phase,* and might have been the most difficult to convince, showed me nothing but unconditional love. "You're my son above all." Coming clean about this part of my life made me feel like we were a family again. No more dark secrets eating away at my soul like the termites that destroyed our dining room set in Antilla. *Mamá, papá, Betty, Tere, I love you.*

A year after we got together, Thom gave me a Cartier ring as symbol of our love. The gesture brought tears to my eyes. Joy and sorrow blended into one. Joy at what the ring represented. Sorrow because memories of *abuelo's* ring, which I had lost at the hands of a revolutionary bastard at Havana airport, flooded my mind. "I'll never take it off," I said. "They'll have to cut my finger off first."

In a way I had come to New York in search of a ring. When I lost *abuelo's*, I lost my music and a part of me. Thom's ring, which I cherish to this day, represented the return of my music, and my commitment to a relationship I never expected I'd have. It also symbolized the return of *abuelo's* hand; the hand that protected and allowed me so many childhood dreams. The little boy from Antilla, the *Pedro Pan* who had come to New York in search of other *muelles* and waters to bring back the magic of innocence, had found his way to a pier of happiness at last.

Although I was a *Pedro Pan* and would always identify myself as such, the Cuban diaspora had other highlights besides *Operación Pedro Pan*. They included immigration through a third country; the Camarioca exodus, which resulted in the Freedom Flights; attempts to escape by any possible means, like the case of the young boy Elián Gonzalez whose desperate journey to freedom included his mother's drowning; and the Mariel boatlift.

The last one referred to a mass exodus of Cubans from Mariel Harbor to the United States between April 15 and October 31, 1980. It was precipitated by a downturn in the Cuban economy which led to more than 10,000 Cubans outside the Peruvian embassy begging for asylum. After that riotous demonstration, Fidel announced that anyone who wanted to leave could do so, and as he did with Camarioca, he chose a point of embarkation, this time Mariel Harbor. The boatlift had negative ramifications for the Carter administration when it became public that some of the 125,000 exiles who had participated in the exodus had been released from Cuban jails and mental-health facilities. The disturbing news resulted in Cubans already in the U.S., including many of my *Pedro Pan* friends and members of my own family, turning their backs to this new group of refugees. I had to admit I too wanted to disassociate myself from this group and was dismayed if someone asked, "Are you a *Marielito?*"

"I'm a *Pedro Pan!*"

If our diaspora spanned decades and involved different economic and social classes, the country we fled, a land of palm trees and sugar cane, linked us all. No matter how we got here, we all shared a dream: to return to a free Cuba. For me, going back became an obsession that burst open like a boil after seeing a documentary called *The Buena Vista Social Club*. A membership organization in Havana, the club held musical events in the 1940s, and fifty years after it closed, a few veteran musicians who had performed during the club's heydays made a recording that became an international success. The group was invited to perform in Amsterdam in 1998 and later at Carnegie Hall in New York City. At Carnegie Hal, the syncopated rhythms that had pulsed through our streets, our mountains and rivers, pulled me toward the island. The country wás not yet free, but the allure to walk to the beat of familiar music on the very grounds where it had originated became impossible to resist. So, four years after the *Buena Vista Social Club* troupe made their New York debut, I returned.

LORENZO PABLO MARTÍNEZ

My high school graduation picture, 1963.

With my mentor Linda Purcell and her husband. On my left is her father.

Jan Fausti, Bonnie's daughter, practicing at WSU.

My dear friend Chuck.

Lorenzo Pablo Martínez

Betty and Tere pretending to lift me. Behind me is the sorority next to our apartment.

Our first Christmas in Pullman as a family.

Carole and I at the Spokane Airport before
I came to New York (1967).

Thom and I shortly after we met.

A hall in the Club San Carlos where I used to perform.

Another view of the same hall at Club San Carlos.

Abuela in Miami celebrating her 91st birthday.

Coda

AT THE train terminal in Havana, the crowd splashed and ebbed as trains came and went. When my train to Santiago was announced, four hours after its scheduled time, I boarded and took my assigned seat next to a window. I was traveling alone; that's how I wanted it. I thought of Thom, Beni, Betty and Tere. Concerned for my safety, they thought me mad for making the trip. "What if they keep you and don't let you come back?" I ignored their warnings. Although I had managed to make sense of life in my adopted country, something in me had always remained behind, sleepwalking in my beloved Santiago (a city I once vowed I'd never leave).

I had spent my first two days in Havana, embracing past and present at once. Time had been unkind to the city; in many instances, only the carcasses remained of places I had frequented as a youngster. The CMQ building where the *Programa de José Antonio Alonso* was taped seemed worn out by age. The mural to the right of the front door so faded, it looked like a painting of prehistoric origin. Thinking El Havanero had walked on the Moorish tiles that covered the entrance, most now cracked, and had been present during my performance in the finals, brought a smile to my face—a feeling of delight that disappeared as soon as I continued my walk.

Establishments, such as *El Fin de Siglo* and other high-end stores, were gone; some razed to the ground by fire; others abandoned and left with broken windows and nothing but empty shelves inside. The neighborhood where these stores once reigned, an area known for its energy and elegance prior to the revolution, had become but a slum. Streets and sidewalks were littered with garbage, water had backed up in gutters and a putrid odor attacked my nostrils with revolutionary fervor. *Fidel, what have you done to my Cuba?*

On my last night in Havana, I attended a performance at the Tropicana, an open-air nightclub that had opened in 1939 on six acres of the city's Marianao's neighborhood and that Fidel had kept open as a tourist attraction. In the early days the shows featured performers such as Xavier Cugat, Carmen Miranda, Nat King Cole, and Josephine Baker. So popular were the shows, that before Castro, Cubana Airlines offered *Tropicana Specials*, round-trip flights from Miami to Havana and back to Florida after the performances ended in the early morning hours. The influence of this night club had infiltrated American television, and in *I Love Lucy*, the character of Ricky Ricardo performed at a fictional Manhattan Tropicana Club, fashioned after the original.

There was no Carmen Miranda or other big names gracing the stage the night I was there. Yet, the show still managed to delight. Statuesque *mulatas* with elaborate headdresses and barely-there costumes paraded their voluptuous curves with alluring appeal—the money the revolution must have spent on sequins and feathers to dress those women could have fed the whole country for weeks, if not months. Sight-gags delivered a good dose of bawdy humor. And as expected, the production culminated in the obligatory conga line, a powerful magnet that drew everyone to their feet.

As the crowded, non-airconditioned train chugged along toward Santiago, I vowed to make peace with my demons, with myself. I looked at the passengers and wondered if they could figure out my story as clearly as I could read theirs based on a phrase I heard here and there. There was the husband, wife and child, returning from a trip to the capital where they had entered the lottery that might win them an exit permit to leave for the United States; the young lovers, taking turns resting their heads on each other's shoulders, now and then sharing a kiss that ended their nap and spoke innocently of a forever adorned with cherubs and bells; the muscular young man, the *jinetero* (hustler) on his way back from a month in Havana, where he made enough money servicing European and Canadian tourists (men and women) to keep him clothed and fed until his next trip.

It was 2002. Far away, in my adopted country, George W. Bush had threatened war with Iraq. The passengers on the train seemed unaware of such danger. I liked them all, the young and the old, the lovers, the sex worker, and even the man in the corner, with the baseball cap and goatee, answering voices that only he could hear (*"Don't tell me to shut up because I haven't said anything to you,"* he would repeat to no one in particular). Was he so different from me? I too had voices I answered, voices that pushed me in this or that direction, *Turn here, no, no, better the other way. Go back, no, no, it might be dangerous.*

I had been warned that as the train made its scheduled stops (Santa Clara, Ciego de Avila, Las Tunas, Alto Cedro), people would get on board and run through the aisles, stealing suitcases from sleepy passengers. Were the people on the train different from the local looters? I wanted to trust them all, but could I? I kept my fingers locked around the handle of my small suitcase, which traveled at my feet. I made sure my ring was not visible.

Creating another nightmare, the train broke down a hundred miles outside of Santiago, and we sat there for more than three hours, waiting for a motorized engine to pull us into the city; the long journey had proven too much for the old mule. Stuck there, I reminisced about my life, which in many ways had played like Beethoven's *Adiós Sonata*. The first movement of my sonata expressed life in Cuba, in Santiago, with a concert and scholarship high-jacked by a telegram. My first *adiós;* the middle movement outlined my exposure to *Operación Pedro Pan,* an *andante* of some playfulness that transitioned with an *adiós* to Matecumbe and landed Beni and me in a questionable *beca;* the third movement opened with an anticipated reunion, which did not provide the personal happiness I expected. Until, with an *adiós* to Carole and Pullman, I went to New York. With my return to Cuba, I was composing a necessary *coda.* Only then I could finish my sonata.

From Santiago's hotel Casa Granda, I knew exactly how to get there: two blocks down to the old Enramada, then right for one block, and a final left for two more. I would pass the Club San Carlos, where my Mozart performance never took place, and *La Casa de Cultura.* I would avoid stopping at either of those buildings. I had something else to do first. For years, I had dreamt of walking through these streets again toward *abuela's* apartment, reveling in the sights, sounds and smells of my old Santiago; each time, I would wake up before arriving at my destination, sweat covering my body, disappointment pounding in my heart.

I turned left onto *calle* Hartmann and had my first glimpse of *abuela's* balcony, which revealed itself shyly, like a virgin shedding her clothes for the first time to a lover. A rail of black Spanish iron embraced the balcony from end to end, the pattern reminiscent of fine lace found in a bride's mantilla. Over it, a marble handrail showed cracks in several places. I worried about pieces falling on passersby.

At that moment, a little girl, her complexion the color of light caramel, appeared on the balcony. She could have been no more than five.

Images of my childhood poured down like torrential rain, washing away the figure of the little girl who, with a smile fixed on her face, claimed the balcony for herself. *The balcony is mine. I'll climb back, take over the balcony, and relive my "trick-the-moon" game. There's been no telegram. I've never left. I'm here. Can't you see? Get out. Get out!*

I stood there frozen by the powerful memories. When the little girl took her smile back inside, I realized I was running late for my visit.

As I turned left onto *calle* Máximo Gómez, Jorge Luis' street, panic played in my head like a discordant symphony. All at once I heard Mozart, still my favorite composer, the impressionists Ravel and Debussy, and even the unmistakable trademark shout of the Cuban Celia Cruz—*Azúcar!* No distinct solos. One melody piled on top of another, edges blurred. A rubble of sounds, a cacophony that continued its musical argument as my steps walked me to Jorge Luís' home.

It was the same dwelling he had lived in with his mother while I was still in Santiago. Same stucco exterior. The yellow paint, however, had softened to a reminder of its past shade. The small square window to the right of the door looked forlorn behind white iron bars. The door was ajar. I knocked.

"*Entra.* Enter!" a voice, whose timber I had not forgotten, said. He was sitting on a wooden rocking chair, one of its arms held in place by a piece of rope. He flashed a smile, but as he got up, his face tightened, distorting his features.

"*¿Qué te pasa?* What's the matter?" I asked.

He mentioned he had a kidney infection and there was no medicine, so he was treating it with homemade remedies.

On an old green couch, arms worn down to the lining, we sat. I to his left, attentive to his every word; the cane on the back of the chair where he sat before was torn.

His mother had passed away, and he was still in the same house but with his wife, Esperanza, and two sons, one a doctor (even he could not get medicine for his father) and the other a teacher.

I wondered what would have happened if I had stayed in Cuba. Would Jorge Luís still have married or would he and I now be sharing this house, broken down furniture and all. "*Te ves muy Americano,*" he told me. He thought I looked American.

Did Jorge Luís really remembered much about us? So much had happened, so many years gone by. He had a family now. I had my own. The same partner for the last thirty years and two dogs—Thom did mean it when he said *forever!* Did Jorge Luís really care to see me, or was I just another of the many refugees returning to Cuba to visit family and friends, bringing presents and dollars they could use in the black market?

"I'm sorry I don't have a piano," he said in warm tones. I told him I hadn't played in a while. I remembered he would come to the *conservatorio* to hear me practice, and images of the two of us danced in front of my eyes: I at the piano, working up a sweat, he on the floor lost in the music of whatever composer I was working on; although sooner or later he'd ask me to play Chopin's *Raindrop Prelude*, his favorite—a composition that starts with a haunting melody and is interrupted by a storm not unlike the one created by the revolution. When the original melody returns, it's almost like a sigh. In many ways, the prelude depicted our lives and, in particular, my relationship with him.

"I had been asked to keep an eye on you, but the proximity also brought out feelings I didn't expect to have for you or...another man," he said.

I shuddered. He continued, "In 1965, Fidel created *las Unidadas Militares para Ayudar a la Producción*. Military Units to Help Production."

I knew about them—their existence another revolution's disgrace. These were camps where young men who were considered unfit for military service were forced into hard labor. Many of them were gays. At that time, the government had asked parents to report children who engaged in homosexual activities, claiming that not doing so was a crime against the revolution. That some parents followed Fidel's mandate and betrayed their own children is still inconceivable to me.

"I was a *miliciano*," Jorge Luís continued. "But I almost ended up in one of those camps as punishment. In the government's eyes I hadn't kept a strict enough eye on you. When you came to me that day, I had to dismiss you. I already knew about your exit permit. The government knows those things. I wanted you to go. The camps were not in place yet, but I was afraid you'd be harmed in some way."

I squirmed in my seat as he closed his eyes. I wasn't sure if the kidney infection or the memories were causing the pain reflected on his face.

"Esperanza knows about you," he said.

I didn't respond.

He took a slow breath, like an asthmatic trying to fill his lungs with oxygen. "The revolution failed you. I failed it as well. What I did with you, they wanted me to do with others. Keep an eye on young men like you to make sure they didn't betray the regime. I couldn't. Not any more."

"*¿Cómo estás ahora?* How are you now?" I asked, my eyes getting moist.

"*La vida aquí es dura.*" Life here is hard. He told me how difficult it was to provide for his family. Even the basic necessities. "Everything is rationed. I'm giving up smoking. My pipe broke. You can only buy them at a Tourist Store. Too much money!" He laughed.

I had spent close to two hours with him and thought he needed rest. I put a one-hundred-dollar bill in his shirt pocket. He took it out, and gave it back. I insisted. "*Un regalito. Para que compres una buena pipa.* A gift. To buy a good pipe." I wasn't sure he would use the money for that, but I didn't care. Perhaps he'd get milk, eggs, chocolate in the black market. Whatever. I wanted to give him something.

He accepted the money, then hugged me. "*Te quiero mucho,*" he said. I didn't tell him I loved him back, because my feelings for him had changed over the years. But, I did say, "*Gracias, muchas gracias.*" The words came easy. I realized how much he had saved me from.

Had I stayed in Cuba, I would have ended up in one of Fidel's forced labor camps. Or, perhaps, arrested at one of the gay bars the regime regularly raided.

Jorge Luis asked me to return the following day for *un Arroz con Pollo* that Esperanza would make. She had gone out to get the chicken—probably a black market bird. I told him I had to catch a flight back to Havana and then New York, which was true. What I didn't tell him was that I was not interested in meeting Esperanza. In fact, I was glad he had managed to have her out while we visited.

One last embrace.

As I looked into his golden-brown eyes, which were swimming in tears, I realized I was not saying goodbye to the man who had endured a difficult time at the hands of his own people, and as a result had acquired a patina of pain on his physical body and soul, but to his younger self: the person who had patiently heard me practice day in day out; the young man who had made me feel like the most important human being in the world; the man whose support had filled me with confidence, even if his encouragement served as a masquerade for his true intentions; the Jorge Luís I thought I could never live without. I could now say *adiós* without anger. I realized that life had happened for both of us the way it was destined, and that our paths had been carved from the beginning, perhaps even before our births, as if in Carrara marble.

After I left Jorge Luís, I visited *el conservatorio* and *Casa de Cultura*. Both produced feelings of nostalgia and euphoria in equal measures. *El conservatorio* brought back memories of my younger self, walking through those creaking floors while a chorale on the courtyard engaged in warm-up exercises *(la, la, la, la, la, la, la)*, and scales, interspersed with the music of Bach or Mozart, rang from one of the practice rooms. In *Casa de Cultura,* I trekked up the majestic staircase with the same youthful enthusiasm I exhibited when I would visit Jorge Luís. As I recalled my last time in this building, the image of an unyielding Jorge Luís standing in the middle of his cluttered office blinded me. It took me a moment to shake off the unpleasant memory, despite his recent words of explanation. When I did, a sense of completion flowed through me—a feeling similar to what I would experience when I finished a musical composition, or at the end of a recital.

Later that night, on the same bench Jorge Luís and I used to occupy, I sat on *Parque Céspedes*, reminiscing about a life that had veered off from the map he had helped me draw. There had been no Prague for me. Instead, I'd had the satisfaction of obtaining master's and doctorate degrees, both in music; hearing my compositions performed at national venues and on television as well as at international festivals; and having books of children's songs published—all inspired by my favorite childhood game:

A mambro cható, materile, rile, rile.

Furthermore, my involvement in the world of non-profits had provided me with an opportunity to give back to those, who, like me and all the other *Pedro Pans* once, needed help.

Behind me that night was *la Catedral*, the angel watching over me. To my right, striped awnings of hotel Casa Granda produced a brightly lit display. In front of me was *el ayuntamiento*. Same white exterior. Same Mediterranean-blue trims. It was one of the few buildings the revolution had maintained, probably because of what it symbolized. As I stared at what I called "Fidel's balcony," I muttered, "Fidel, *History will not absolve you.* You have destroyed my country. I will not return until Cuba is no longer oppressed by you and your *Communist* dictatorship."

It was time to pack my bags. As I walked the few yards to Casa Granda, I heard one of the songs made popular by the group *Buena Vista Social Club* coming from the hotel terrace. Stars glowed in the sky, in a pattern so random and whimsical, it could have been the art work of a child. My steps marked the rhythm of the song. I took one last peek at the evening sky and saw the moon, a bright disc that had been there since my childhood, following me, listening to my secrets. That night it would hear something I could finally say aloud, goodbye. To Santiago. Jorge Luís. Cuba.

Cuba, my precious Cuba, *Adiós*.

Operación Pedro Pan

OPERACIÓN PEDRO PAN has often been compared to the *Kindertransport,* a rescue mission prior to the outbreak of World War II that saved more than 10,000 German children from the Holocaust.

The origin of *Operación Pedro Pan* can be traced to a meeting in Miami between James Baker and Father Walsh. Baker had been director of the Ruston Academy, a school for Havana's elite. The academy was closed when Fidel shut down all schools to start an educational reform. Baker, an American who had lived in Cuba for many years, was asked by teachers of the academy and parents of former students to help them get their children out of Cuba.

Baker and Father Walsh devised a plan, thinking they would be dealing at the most with two hundred children whose stay in this country would be temporary. But the number grew and between 1960 and 1962, more than 14,000 Cuban minors had come to this country as part of *Operación Pedro Pan.* The program initially received support from Miami-operated businesses and later from the U.S. government.

Some people attributed the name of the program to an experience Father Bryan O. Walsh had when a Cuban, a boy, alone and wandering the streets of Miami, came to his office in need of assistance. His name was Pedro Menéndez.

"Pan for Pedro, Pan for Pedro." Pan was the euphemism for bread or help. He was one of the first Cuban boys Father Walsh came in contact with; the meeting with James Baker had not taken place yet.

Others believed the name derived from *Peter Pan*, J.M. Barrie's classic children's story that featured the adventures of a boy by the same name who refused to grow up. With a gang of Lost Boys, Peter flew around Neverland, interacting with mermaids, fairies, pirates; occasionally meeting ordinary children from the world outside. This is perhaps the most popular attribution, for those in the program were lost children, flying from Cuba to a land of hope and plenty, where fairy tales came true (at least for some).

He might have been unaware of the name by which his program would eventually become known, but clarity of vision, risks and all, had underlined Walsh's plan from the start. To keep the Cuban regime unaware of the exodus of those children, Father Walsh worked through a network composed of individual clergy in Cuba and some prominent figures of the counterrevolution rather than the official Church body in the country.

Through that elaborate network, Cuban children received the necessary documentation to enter the U. S., a Visa Waiver instead of a standard visa, and proof that they had been accepted to an American school; the latter a fictitious document. Even the dollars needed in Cuba to buy plane tickets reached the hands of parents whose children had received visas. So it was that thousands of children came to America with the pretext of a scholarship to an American school. It was a ruse to keep Fidel unaware of the real purpose of these children's departure, which begged the question, how could Fidel ignore such a large exodus of youngsters going abroad to study?

Walsh's efforts, which eventually became known as *Operación Pedro Pan,* had the blessing of the U. S. government. The Eisenhower administration offered financial support and agreed to grant visas to children up to sixteen years of age. Walsh, himself, was allowed to issue visas to older children up to eighteen as long as he cleared the names with the State Department. When Kennedy took office, he continued to support this program.

Because Walsh insisted that while here these children receive the same religious nurturing they had at home, he turned to the Jewish Family and Children's Service to assist children of the Jewish faith, and to the Children's Service Bureau to care for all unaccompanied Protestant Cuban children. When children arrived at the Miami airport, they were asked what religious denomination they belonged to and assigned to the proper group. Because most of the youngsters coming out of Cuba, however, were Catholic, the heaviest burden fell on the Catholic Welfare Bureau.

Under its aegis, several camps operated in Miami. Matecumbe served as shelter for boys aged fourteen to eighteen; Kendall, initially a transit center for girls, turned into a facility for boys ages twelve to fourteen; Florida City, became a site for girls of all ages and boys up to twelve; St. Raphael, as well as the Jesuit-run Whitehall, both havens for "lucky boys," were also part of the *Pedro Pan* program.

As the number of arrivals grew swiftly, Monsignor was pressured to move these children out as soon as possible from a city that already had a large Cuban population. He reached out to Catholic dioceses and social service agencies across the country, and although many children found refuge in private homes, some ended up in orphanages or reform schools where conditions were a far cry from what they experienced at home. Most of these children came from middle- to upper-class families, pampered environments that contrasted with the rough and tumble situations they found in institutions housing criminal or violent youth. The only crime these Cuban children had committed was coming to this country as refugees, and not knowing English, which in some instances caused them to receive severe beatings from clergy and teachers who believed these children were stupid or refusing to learn the language. How could anyone lie to our parents, to us, about what awaited us here?

The answers to those questions are as varied as the number of children who participated in the program. Most of the *Pedro Pan* boys and girls, regardless of their experience, felt grateful for the opportunity they had to come to a country where they could lead a life of freedom.

This book is an account of my personal story. An individual tale. For a comprehensive description of the *Pedro Pan* program, before, during and after the Missile Crisis, I recommend, *The Lost Apple* by María de los Angeles Torres, published by Beacon Press; *Operación Pedro Pan* by Yvonne M. Conde, published by Random House; and *Fleeing Castro: Operation Pedro Pan and the Cuban Children's Program* by Victor Andres Triay, published by University Press of Florida. These publications served as resources during the writing of my book, helping to clarify events that time had turned vague in my mind.

Acknowledgement

THERE ARE SO many people to thank. First and foremost, my dear friend Lara Tabac, who believed in me and unbeknownst to me, showed my writing to literary agent Alison Bond. Alison agreed to represent me and has been involved in every phase of this book's journey. Thank you both. Your friendship and support have enriched my life in myriad ways.

Several people read portions of an early version of the manuscript and offered helpful advice. Among them are Patricia Fisher, Barbara Case Senchak and Sherrye Henry. Their encouragement kept me going, particularly when inspiration faltered.

My appreciation to editor Jane Rosenman, who pointed me in the right direction, and to everyone involved in the production of this book: Ciro Flores, a gifted artist who designed the cover, and José Saenz, who worked tirelessly preparing the files for publication, both the digital version and the print format.

Deserving thanks also is my online writing group, an outgrowth of an online writing class led by Lori Wilde, a prolific author who after our first assignment told me, "You should write a memoir." Two members of the group stand out, for they were there with feedback no matter how many times I turned to them. They are Susan Bernhardt, gifted mystery writer, and Dave Bazan, wittiest man I know, whose comments as well as his comedy scripts always made me laugh. And laughter I needed as I labored to bring this book to life. I can't thank them enough.

Other friends who offered valuable insight and support throughout the writing of this book are Dr. Agnes Wilkie, Dr. Scott Roggue, Joan Reynolds, Carol Anne Brown, Kathy Pooler, Carol Wyatt, Sallie Woodell, Marielena Aguilera and Manrique Iriarte.

My family was supportive as well. My brother helped with his own recollections of the time I write about; my sisters offered their own experience leaving Cuba; and my father left me nine typed, single-spaced pages—computer were not in vogue yet— of what he and my mother had experienced in Mexico.

A special thanks to Teresa Laughlin, long-time mentor who had been after me for years to write this book.

My deepest thanks to my love and life partner, Thom Cunningham, who never tired of reading "one more version", "one more section." I benefitted from his critical eye and insightful comments. Thank you, Thom, for understanding every time I said no to a movie or dinner, because I had work to do. I needed your unselfishness while I obsessed with completing this project. Without your support this memoir would have never been written.

I am also indebted to Yvonne M. Conde for her *Operation Pedro Pan: The Untold Exodus of 14,048 Cuban Children* (Routledge, 2000); and to Maria Torres for *The Lost Apple: Operation Pedro Pan, Cuban Children in the U.S., and the Promise of a Better Future* (Beacon Press, 2004). Both excellent resources helped me clarify points that had become fuzzy over the years.

To all the Pedro Pans, I extend a warm *gracias*. They served as my inspiration. I hope to have honored their valor and dignity.

About The Author

BORN IN CUBA, Lorenzo Pablo Martínez was part of *Operación Pedro Pan,* a secretive mass exodus of children fleeing the Castro regime that landed in America between 1960 and 1962. He holds a master's in piano performance from the Manhattan School of Music and a doctorate in music education from Teachers College, Columbia University. As a pianist, he has appeared in recitals and on radio and television. His musical compositions have been performed nationally and at international festivals. The television show *Captain Kangaroo* featured some of his works, and for *Group Soup,* a children's book published by Viking, he contributed the title song. In addition, a book of his children's songs, *The Circus,* was published by Clarus Music Ltd.

Lorenzo Pablo Martinez translated all twelve episodes of *The Second Voyage of the Mimi* produced by Bank Street College of Education for PBS, and published his own children's story, *The Ballerina and the Peanut Butter and Jelly Sandwich.* He co-edited *The Ginseng Conspiracy,* a mystery by Susan Bernhardt, published by Muse It Up. His memoir, *CUBA, ADIÓS,* explores his *Pedro Pan* experience. Martinez is currently working on a second memoir and a Young Adult mystery novel.

Over the years Martínez has played important roles in the not-for-profit arena, overseeing the development and communications/marketing departments for a number of international organizations specializing in health and women's rights. He has represented those organizations at international conferences and has been a lecturer at several New York institutions such as New York University, the New School, York College of the City University of New York and the 92nd Street Y.

Made in the USA
Lexington, KY
10 July 2018